"Howlett and Rademacher provide an invaluab
academic coaching. Discussions of topics rangii
academic coaching to specific strategies for effectively coaching students from
all demographics provide a clearly written roadmap for staff and faculty focused
on preparing students to become independent life-long learners."

Saundra McGuire, *Louisiana State University, USA*

"*Academic Coaching* is a must-read for all who are concerned with supporting
student success in higher education…Marc A. Howlett and Kristen Rademacher
are two of the foremost leaders in the academic coaching field and they know their
subject well. They participated in the development of one of the first and most
highly recognized academic coaching programs in the country. In addition, they
both have years of practical experience coaching college students. This book provides a comprehensive resource on academic coaching taking readers from theory
and research to the practical skills of how to have a coaching conversation. If you
are looking for ways to help college students be more successful within the array
of challenges that are facing them, this is a book you need to read."

Sharon Field, *Wayne State University, USA*

"*Academic Coaching* is a powerful guide to providing evidence-based coaching on
your campus. Marc and Kristen are masterful coaches as well as highly skilled
trainers. Like their remarkable workshops, this publication comfortably but
comprehensively guides the reader in using coaching mindset and techniques
to promote student engagement and academic success. They have integrated
various approaches that will be familiar to postsecondary service providers and
faculty members who want to support student learning but keep their work
squarely within the unique realm of coaching. This book will quickly become
your go-to for launching or strengthening your academic success coaching
services."

David R. Parker, *Children's Resource Group, USA*

"A thoughtful and accessible model for empowering students to achieve goals.
This book carefully presents the nuts and bolts of a coaching framework that can
be quickly adapted by anyone and calibrated for any educational institution."

Jay Sriram, *Washington University in St. Louis, USA*

"*Academic Coaching* is a practical guide for any higher education professional
working in a coaching or advising role. The concepts and methods outlined in
this book work in career coaching as well. Career coaches benefit from this
model because it's practical in nature but grounded in research. All higher
education coaches and advisors should add this to their professional library."

Sue Harbour, *University of California, Berkeley, USA*

Academic Coaching

Academic Coaching is the first comprehensive book about academic coaching in higher education, providing faculty and staff with a robust foundation in academic coaching that they can use to improve campus services to bolster student success.

Drawing from the principles of executive, business, and life coaching, this book explores how to support college students as they begin their journey to independence, grapple with challenging courses, uncover their life's purpose, and prepare to make their mark on the world.

This accessible book is full of step-by-step guidance for becoming an effective academic coach, helping faculty and staff create, expand, incorporate, or improve academic coaching services on campus in order to better serve all students.

Marc A. Howlett, PhD, CPCC, is the Assistant Director at the Learning Center at the University of North Carolina at Chapel Hill, USA.

Kristen Rademacher, MEd, CPCC, PCC, is an ADHD/LD Specialist at the Learning Center at the University of North Carolina at Chapel Hill, USA.

Academic Coaching

Coaching College Students for Success

Marc A. Howlett
Kristen Rademacher

Routledge
Taylor & Francis Group

NEW YORK AND LONDON

Designed cover image: © Getty Images

First published 2023
by Routledge
605 Third Avenue, New York, NY 10158

and by Routledge
4 Park Square, Milton Park, Abingdon, Oxon, OX14 4RN

Routledge is an imprint of the Taylor & Francis Group, an informa business

Library of Congress Cataloging-in-Publication Data
Names: Howlett, Marc A., author. | Rademacher, Kristen, author.
Title: Academic coaching: coaching college students for success /
Marc A. Howlett & Kristen Rademacher.
Description: New York, NY: Routledge, 2023. |
Includes bibliographical references. |
Identifiers: LCCN 2022053902 (print) | LCCN 2022053903 (ebook) |
ISBN 9781032265711 (hardback) | ISBN 9781032272214 (paperback) |
ISBN 9781003291879 (ebook)
Subjects: LCSH: Counseling in higher education. | Faculty advisors.
Classification: LCC LB2343 .H65 2023 (print) |
LCC LB2343 (ebook) | DDC 378.1/9422—dc23/eng/20230221
LC record available at https://lccn.loc.gov/2022053902
LC ebook record available at https://lccn.loc.gov/2022053903

ISBN: 978-1-032-26571-1 (hbk)
ISBN: 978-1-032-27221-4 (pbk)
ISBN: 978-1-003-29187-9 (ebk)

DOI: 10.4324/9781003291879

Typeset in Perpetua
by codeMantra

To the incredible college students we have the privilege of coaching every day.

Contents

Preface

We wrote this book to meet a need. While academic coaching has been part of higher education for over 20 years, there are few published resources on the subject. We have extensive professional experience providing academic coaching to college students, delivering academic coaching trainings, and researching academic coaching. Over the years, in different settings and contexts we kept hearing "What book on academic coaching would you recommend?" While there are many excellent books on life coaching and ADHD coaching and there are tremendous volumes on topics like learning study strategies, when it came to academic coaching in higher education we couldn't point to a specific book.

So we wrote one.

This book is informed by our collective decades of professional academic coaching experience. We endeavored to write a thorough yet accessible guide to academic coaching in higher education based on direct practice, theoretical frameworks, and empirical research. Most importantly, we aimed to create a resource to help interested staff and faculty learn the principles and practices of academic coaching so they could coach college students for success. After all, our professional mission is to help college students identify, work toward, and then achieve their academic goals.

Academic coaching, of course, as well as our efforts to systematically chronicle it within the pages of this book, developed within much broader contexts than us two authors. We are professional academic coaches at the Writing and Learning Center at the University of North Carolina-Chapel Hill, a university that has offered forms of college coaching for more than two decades. We would like to express our gratitude for the contributions, especially of our current and former colleagues, without whom this book would not have been possible.

First, we'd like to thank Jane Benson, the former Director of the department previously titled Learning Disabilities Services. Jane was the first person at UNC-Chapel Hill who opened the door to academic coaching when she'd sought improved ways to support students with ADHD and learning differences. Her tenacious leadership laid the foundation for the eventually transformed pedagogy in which academic support staff at our university now works with students.

Next, we are deeply indebted to Dr. Theresa Laurie Maitland, our former colleague at the Writing and Learning Center. Jane Benson handed the coaching baton to Theresa after she'd left UNC-Chapel Hill in 2005. For the decade-plus that followed, Theresa worked tirelessly to support our growing staff in the adoption of coaching. A masterful coach herself, Theresa impacted the lives of thousands of students she coached and was a role model for each new staff member who joined the team. A leader in the field of ADHD and learning differences, Theresa co-authored three books on the topic and co-authored peer-reviewed journal articles on coaching's efficacy. In her final years at the Writing and Learning Center, Theresa co-developed and co-delivered a coaching training as part of a broad effort to bring the coach approach method of working with students to the larger university community. The seeds for this book were planted by Theresa years ago, and her influence and wisdom are present throughout its pages.

We're grateful for the support and leadership of Dr. Marcus Collins, Associate Dean and Director of the Center for Student Success, and Dr. Abigail Panter, Senior Associate Dean of the Office of Undergraduate Education. We truly appreciate the positive cheerleading Dean Collins broadcasts about academic coaching in his collaborations with UNC-Chapel Hill administrators across campus.

We are thankful for the leadership of Dr. Kim Abels, Director of the Writing and Learning Center. Kim's expertise in writing center pedagogy and administration provided a foundation for making a coach approach the overarching model of working with college students at our center. Kim supported efforts to systematize the training for all staff, which has improved the overall caliber of academic coaching.

We are incredibly lucky to work with a great group of supportive colleagues. They inspire us with their skill and dedication. We are better coaches because of them. A sincere thank you to Robin Blanton, Jackie Stone, Lara Edwards, Robin Horton, Ben Carpenter, Alex Funt, Warren Christian, Gigi Taylor, Franny Brock, Sarah Miller Esposito, Kim Haith, Luke Fayard, Victoria Chavis, and Tierra Williams.

We are also grateful to have been able to collaborate with and learn from many other professionals. From former colleagues within the Writing and Learning Center, to our campus partners in the School of Education and the Office of Undergraduate Education, to our talented graduate student coaches (with an extra thanks to Conor O'Neill and Melissa McWilliams for their research support), to our former Co-Active® Training Institute (CTI) leaders, and to friends we've made at professional conferences through the years: we thank them all.

Their work has influenced our coaching with students and has improved the coaching training we deliver.

At Routledge, we'd like to specifically thank Heather Jarrow for her support in making this book a reality.

Lastly, we'd like to express our gratitude to our friends and family. Kristen appreciates Bill's patience, which has made writing this book possible, and his sense of humor, which makes everything in her life better. And Marc thanks Laurie, Ezra, and Bronx for their loyalty and motivational support to bring this book to completion.

Chapter 1

Introduction

Academic coaching is hot. Colleges and universities are hiring academic coaches and developing coaching programs. In many institutions, existing student support programs are being rebranded and reconfigured as academic coaching. The Association for the Coaching and Tutoring Profession (ACTP) offers academic coaching certification. Higher education conferences regularly feature academic coaching presentations and workshops. And empirical research on academic coaching is becoming much more common.

But when you poke into the subject a little, the field of academic coaching is rather fuzzy. The term academic coaching can be utilized in a variety of ways, and there is little consensus about what it means (Robinson, 2015). There is a nascent but burgeoning research literature on academic coaching, but few published resources exist for university staff, faculty, and administrators.

That's where this book comes in. The purpose of this book is to provide a comprehensive practical guide to academic coaching for higher education professionals. *Academic Coaching: Coaching College Students for Success* can be used by current academic coaches as a resource to bolster their work, by colleges aiming to initiate or expand academic coaching services, and by a range of university staff and faculty wanting to make their interpersonal work with students more effective. Reading this book and applying its contents will help you acquire academic coaching skills immediately applicable to your work with college students. You'll learn how to facilitate academic conversations that effectively promote student growth and independence.

WHY ACADEMIC COACHING? WHY NOW? WHY US?

To answer these questions, we need to start with a brief definition. At its core, academic coaching is a method of facilitating a structured conversation that helps students set, make progress on, and achieve their unique academic goals. Academic coaching enables college students to take charge of all aspects of their

DOI: 10.4324/9781003291879-1

academic lives. Academic coaching is holistic and individualized and emphasizes non-hierarchical communication and collaboration between the coach and the student. Our sessions are tailored to meet students wherever they are on their academic journey. Academic coaching is valuable to a wide range of students and cultivates an empowering set of attitudes and strategies to serve them in college and their futures.

We maintain that academic coaching in higher education represents something new and is not merely a rebranding of services that may have existed for years or even decades. A primary element of this novel approach is the formalized application of life coaching principles, methods, and structures within the context of academic support in higher education. Academic coaching largely emerged and was adapted from the world of life and executive coaching. Indeed, we received our foundational coaching training and certification from the Co-Active® Training Institute (CTI). Their training and book inspired many aspects of this academic coaching model (Kimsey-House et al., 2018).

Academic coaching is expansive and individualized. Here are a few examples of students who've sought out and benefited from our academic coaching:

- Svati, describing herself as drowning in hundreds of pages of reading, spent every waking moment with her books.
- A STEM honors student taking a full load of classes, Jenny faced a two-week span with four papers and five exams.
- Alex returned to the university after a multi-year absence. Determined to get back into good academic standing, they arrived to academic coaching on the first day of the semester.
- Desmond found it difficult to form study groups with classmates he didn't know, feeling isolated as the only Black student in his math class.
- While trying to complete his PhD, Marc continued to set deadlines with his advisor only to repeatedly miss them.
- Recently diagnosed with ADHD, Julia described her relationship with time at college as nonexistent.
- Heather, a first-generation college student from a rural town, felt unsure about how to go about fulfilling her professor's feedback of "joining the academic conversation."

While academic coaching for college students is relatively new, the University of North Carolina-Chapel Hill has offered forms of coaching to college students since the late 1990s (Byron & Parker, 2002; Parker & Byron, 1998; Quinn et al., 2000). Shortly after the new millennium, our colleague, Dr. Theresa Maitland, became a Certified Professional Co-Active Coach (CPCC) through CTI. Kristen followed a few years later, and they further adapted and expanded principles and approaches from their training to work with college students with ADHD and learning differences. After Kristen and Theresa became part of the Learning Center at UNC-Chapel Hill, the academic coaching program expanded to become available to all undergraduate students. See Chapter 2 for a more detailed account of the growth of academic coaching in higher education.

We wrote this book building on our extensive professional work at one of the international leaders in higher education academic coaching, the UNC-Chapel Hill Writing and Learning Center. We have decades of experience providing academic coaching to thousands of college students. Marc, who is the relative newcomer, has been a college academic coach since 2014. We conduct coaching trainings for staff and faculty at UNC-Chapel Hill, at other universities, and at national conferences. We research, present, and publish on higher education academic coaching including peer-reviewed articles on the effects of academic coaching on college students (Howlett, McWilliams, Rademacher, O'Neill, et al., 2021; Richman et al., 2014) and academic coaching training on university professionals (Howlett et al., 2017; Howlett, McWilliams, Rademacher, Maitland, et al., 2021). Our goal in writing this book is to provide a resource to other higher education professionals who want to expand or incorporate academic coaching into their work.

HOW TO USE THIS BOOK

Academic Coaching: Coaching College Students for Success is divided into four parts. Part One traces the historical growth of academic coaching from its roots in the world of life coaching to becoming a widespread form of academic support (Chapter 2). Interweaved within the discussion of the evolution of academic coaching in higher education will be a brief review of scholarly literature. In this part, we'll also examine several of the practices and theoretical foundations that inform academic coaching.

Part Two describes a full model of academic coaching. While a variety of approaches can be taken to reading this book, we highly recommend that everyone reads Part Two. The academic coaching model presented here consists of a thorough definition of academic coaching (Chapter 3), the fundamental beliefs we as academic coaches hold about the students with whom we work (Chapter 4), the fundamental tools an academic coach uses when working with students (Chapter 5), the four phases of an academic coaching conversation (Chapter 6), and a set of expanded academic coaching skills (Chapter 7). Part Two concludes with two extended case studies that illustrate the many components of the academic coaching model working together (Chapter 8).

Part Three focuses on applying academic coaching in multiple higher education settings and with different student populations. We discuss some of the most common topics within academic coaching (Chapter 9). We look at how faculty/instructors and college staff (e.g., academic advisers, career counselors,

3

academic support staff, accessibility services staff) can apply academic coaching skills in their professional work (Chapters 10 and 11). Part Three also examines academic coaching when working with a great diversity of college students (Chapter 12). Finally, we detail how the academic coaching model can be implemented for remote and virtual interactions with students (Chapter 13).

Part Four lays out a framework of steps higher education professionals can take to apply some or many elements of academic coaching to their work (Chapter 14). This section also contains ideas for academic coaching training activities.

Throughout the book, the principles and applications of academic coaching will be illustrated with examples of sessions with students. These snapshots and snippets of conversations help bring the coaching to life as well as provide examples of academic coaching applications. Except for the extended example below, each student is fictional, although their situations are based on authentic conversations we've had with students over the years.

LET'S MEET JACOB

Jacob is a former student who used academic coaching regularly. His story will give you a glimpse of the scope of topics students can bring to a conversation. Jacob's coaching experience illustrates the collaborative, strengths-based nature of academic coaching.

Upon meeting him as a first-year student, it became immediately apparent that Jacob was unusually bright with a high degree of self-awareness. He was also overwhelmed, juggling extracurriculars, adjusting to life away from home, and meeting the demands of rigorous classes. Jacob felt stressed and was attempting to stay afloat when he began academic coaching, so through the collaborative coaching process he decided that getting organized was a critical first goal. Specifically, Jacob wanted to turn in assignments on time, prepare for midterms and finals, and stop running himself ragged. Snapshots of initial sessions show Jacob and his coach collaborating on:

- Sketching out highly structured daily and weekly plans to help Jacob transition from one task to the next
- Listing all the steps needed to write lengthy papers from start to finish, with Jacob scheduling a timeline to draft each step
- Creating target bedtimes to get enough sleep, with Jacob setting alerts on his phone to remind him when to start wrapping up the evening

At the start of Jacob's sophomore year, he returned to academic coaching with new goals in mind. He wanted to create a sustainable schedule for himself to make effective and meaningful use of his time. Because his classes were sprinkled throughout the week, Jacob wanted to plan how to use time between classes productively and proactively. He also wanted to exercise regularly. Most importantly, he desired to minimize the frazzled feeling that characterized much of his first year. Jacob's academic coaching sessions focused on helping him develop a planning routine to promote thriving and not just surviving. Jacob decided to implement Sunday planning sessions to review upcoming assignments and tasks and map out a corresponding study schedule, including when he would exercise and socialize. Because Jacob knew that he had strength in visual learning, he purchased a large whiteboard for his room and used it to keep an ongoing, detailed, color-coded list of to-dos. Jacob still became stressed during the busy midterm and final exam weeks, but his new planning systems provided him with better tools to navigate a semester's ebb and flow.

After Jacob expanded his skills to manage and organize himself, a new theme emerged in his academic coaching sessions: preparing and positioning himself for long-term goals. As a sophomore, Jacob had a notion of working in public health, medicine, or both. However, his humanities-based classes thus far had not made him a competitive candidate to gain entrance into either field. A series of academic coaching sessions in which Jacob talked through his attraction to these fields, particularly public health, ultimately led Jacob to discover that he could design his own multi-disciplinary major. He then created a unique pathway to becoming a competitive candidate for a graduate program. The scope of Jacob's future coursework began to take shape, which provided an anchor for the rest of his undergraduate career. For example, whenever Jacob needed a motivational jolt when grappling with a challenging class assignment, he reminded himself of his long-term professional goals.

Junior year brought new challenges, namely a set of demanding upper-level classes. Jacob's initial difficulties had mostly been around time management and organization. However, he now found himself in classes that required advanced study skills and a higher degree of independent learning. Goals in his academic coaching sessions reflected these priorities, and he focused on reframing his reduced academic confidence as an opportunity to develop more sophisticated learning strategies and approaches. One outcome of this challenging year was his realization that he needed to dramatically improve notetaking in lectures and reading. Jacob developed a vision for using his notes to better prepare him for class, papers, and exams. With this vision in mind, Jacob began experimenting with a notetaking program on his tablet. By the end of his junior year, Jacob had designed a notetaking method that leveraged the power of a digital platform and brought him academic success in his classes.

Jacob continued to use academic coaching throughout his senior year and had become even more adept at using his sessions advantageously. He came to meetings prepared with agenda items, ranging from creating a study plan for a busy week ahead to networking with professors in public health fields to reflecting on his overall growth as a student. By the time Jacob neared graduation, his goals for life after college came into focus. Before applying to graduate school, where he hopes to earn dual MD-MPH degrees, Jacob would first volunteer for national service opportunities as well as pursue post-baccalaureate programs. Jacob marshaled the resources needed to complete his busy senior year while simultaneously designing a detailed blueprint for his next steps after graduation. Considering that Jacob's initial academic coaching sessions focused on developing foundational planning and organizational skills, his approach to academics and being a student had been transformational.

Jacob's experiences reflect academic coaching's overall aim, which is to promote student learning and growth over time. The iterative process of academic coaching provided Jacob with the space to reflect on his strengths and needs, the guidance to explore strategies, and the tools to design meaningful action plans. He is well on his way. What a privilege to accompany students like Jacob on their path to learn new academic skills and strategies, deepen their self-understanding, and point themselves in the direction of their long-term goals and dreams.

When asked to reflect on academic coaching, Jacob shared,

> The coaching process is really iterative and gives me an awesome ability to try things out and see how they work for me and my specific learning style.... Coaching has helped me confront roadblocks by not looking at them as things standing in my path, but as opportunities to change how I am using my study resources and my time... Coaching has given me ways of approaching problems, not just for a particular problem, but for other scenarios that may be similar in the future as well.

REFERENCES

Byron, J., & Parker, D. R. (2002). College students with ADHD: New challenges and directions. In L. C. Brinckerhoff, J. M. McGuire, & S. F. Shaw (Eds.), *Postsecondary education and transition for students with learning disabilities* (2nd ed., pp. 335–387). PRO-ED, Inc.

Howlett, M. A., Maitland, T. L., Rademacher, K., O'Neill, J. C., McWilliams, M. A., Abels, K., Demetriou, C., & Panter, A. T. (2017). *An academic coaching approach for faculty and staff: Professional development and student support.* Annual Convention of the American Psychological Association, Washington, D.C.

Howlett, M. A., McWilliams, M. A., Rademacher, K., Maitland, T. L., O'Neill, J. C., Abels, K., Demetriou, C., & Panter, A. (2021). An academic coaching training program for university professionals: A mixed methods examination. *Journal of Student Affairs Research and Practice, 58*(3), 335–349. https://doi.org/10.1080/19 496591.2020.1784750

Howlett, M. A., McWilliams, M. A., Rademacher, K., O'Neill, J. C., Maitland, T. L., Abels, K., Demetriou, C., & Panter, A. T. (2021). Investigating the effects of academic coaching on college students' metacognition. *Innovative Higher Education*, 46(2), 189–204. https://doi.org/10.1007/s10755-020-09533-7

Kimsey-House, H., Kimsey-House, K., Sandahl, P., & Whitworth, L. (2018). *Co-Active Coaching: The proven framework for transformative conversations at work and life* (4th ed.). Nicholas Brealey Publishing.

Parker, D. R., & Byron, J. (1998). Differences between college students with LD and AD/HD: Practical implications for service providers. In P. O. Quinn & A. McCormick (Eds.), *Re-thinking AD/HD: A guide to fostering success in students with AD/HD at the college level* (pp. 14–30). Advantage Books.

Quinn, P. O., Ratey, N., & Maitland, T. L. (2000). *Coaching college students with AD/HD: Issues and answers*. Advantage Books.

Richman, E. L., Rademacher, K. N., & Maitland, T. L. (2014). Coaching and college success. *Journal of Postsecondary Education and Disability*, 27(1), 33–50. https://files.eric.ed.gov/fulltext/EJ1029647.pdf

Robinson, C. E. (2015). *Academic/success coaching: A description of an emerging field in higher education* [PhD Thesis]. University of South Carolina.

Part I

Background and Research

Chapter 2

Growth of Academic Coaching

While it seems fair to say that academic coaching is a relatively new form of student support in higher education, at least in terms of broad usage, the overall profession of coaching dates back much earlier. We maintain that college academic coaching represents something new and is not simply a rebranding of previous academic support services such as tutoring or study skills instruction. What makes academic coaching different is the framework of coaching.

In this chapter, we provide a quick history of academic coaching in higher education, including its growth at the University of North Carolina-Chapel Hill. As part of that story, we highlight empirical research on college academic coaching. The second half of the chapter consists of brief examinations of concurrent developments, both programmatic and theoretical, that inform and inspire academic coaching.

ORIGINS

Sports and Life Coaching

Sports coaching is the origin of all forms of coaching. In essence, the role of a sports coach is to help athletes grow their skills and abilities to optimize their performance. While the athletes train, coaches guide, encourage, offer feedback, provide accountability, and cheer them on from the sidelines during competitions.

One doesn't have to stretch their imagination too far to see how the essence of sports coaching would be beneficial to those in arenas beyond athletics. Having an ally to help define and progress toward personal or professional goals? Building better habits through accountability and encouragement? Receiving the space and guidance to reflect on and evaluate your growth? Sounds wonderful, right?

Life coaching and other professional forms of coaching were inspired by sports coaching but with some key differences. Life coaching is generally more

DOI: 10.4324/9781003291879-3

11

collaborative and less prescriptive than sports coaching. The development of life coaching as a professional field saw tremendous growth in the 1980s and into the 1990s. Laura Whitworth, Karen Kimsey-House, and Henry Kimsey-House founded the Coaches Training Institute (CTI) in 1992 (Co-Active Training Institute, n.d.). Three years later, Thomas Leonard founded the International Coaching Federation (ICF), an independent professional organization for the field (International Coaching Federation, n.d.-a).

According to ICF "coaching is partnering in a thought-provoking and creative process that inspires a person to maximize their personal and professional potential" (International Coaching Federation, n.d.-b). In contrast to mentoring, consulting, or therapy, "coaching focuses on facilitating individuals or groups to draw upon their own experiences and capabilities to set and reach their own objectives" (International Coaching Federation, n.d.-b). Unlike other practices, especially in clinical settings, where the client is meant to be diagnosed and made better by experts, in coaching the client has the most expertise.

One common form of life coaching consists of the GROW model (Alexander & Renshaw, 2005; O'Connor & Lages, 2007; Spence & Grant, 2007; Whitmore, 2017). GROW is an acronym that stands for Goal, Options, Reality, and What's Next. The GROW model is a practical framework characterized by intentional forward momentum and growth. And since the model operates within the broader framework of coaching, it is based on collaborative relationships where the coachee, not the professional coach, retains the agency for setting their goals and then achieving them.

By the turn of the millennium, professional coaching became a booming, international industry. The demand for more training programs grew, and success stories abounded from those who'd received this form of coaching. Professional and personal coaching were here to stay. And right around the start of the twenty-first century was when coaching went to college.

Coaching Enters the Academy

There is no definitive account of when and how academic coaching entered higher education, but evidence converges to the late 1990s. In 2000, a private organization named InsideTrack began providing academic coaching services to numerous public and private universities with an emphasis on undergraduate retention (Bettinger & Baker, 2014, p. 6). One early account of these efforts cited improving graduation rates as the impetus for bringing academic coaching to campus with support for first-generation college students being especially important (Farrell, 2007). A randomized control trial study of these coaching services with a sample of over 13,000 undergraduates found positive and significant effects of academic coaching on student retention and persistence (Bettinger & Baker, 2014). The Bettinger and Baker study continues to be one of the most important and frequently cited contributions to the academic coaching research literature.

Another major entry point for coaching into higher education consisted of services for students with ADHD, which is how academic coaching began at our institution, the University of North Carolina at Chapel Hill. In the mid-1990s, interested by the growing popularity of ADHD coaching in private practices, a group of professional staff within UNC-Chapel Hill's Learning Disability Services (LDS) office including Jane Benson, Dr. David Parker, and Dr. Theresa Maitland began exploring and adapting elements of life coaching to work with college students (Byron & Parker, 2002; Parker & Byron, 1998). By 1997, UNC-Chapel Hill was formally offering "college coaching" to students with ADHD, a service presented as "a working relationship in which an LDS staff member helps you identify and reach short-term academic goals that you are committed to working on" (Byron & Parker, 2002, p. 376). While UNC-Chapel Hill played a critical role in developing and expanding college ADHD coaching, efforts were also underway at other universities exploring coaching as a service to support students with ADHD (Byron & Parker, 2002; Zwart & Kallemeyn, 2001).

Providing ADHD coaching to college students had become a large enough phenomenon by the late 1990s that UNC-Chapel Hill's Dr. Theresa Maitland co-authored a book on the subject (Quinn et al., 2000). Sue Sussman of the American Coaching Association wrote in the book's foreward that "coaching is a vehicle for helping individuals become successful, according to their own definition of 'success'—an admirable goal for any educational institution, whether it be Hatboro Elementary School or Harvard University" (2000, p. ix). An overarching goal of academic coaching, helping students achieve success as they define it, remains the same more than two decades after that writing.

The formalization and establishment of academic coaching for college students at UNC-Chapel Hill advanced in the early 2000s when Dr. Theresa Maitland became a trained, certified coach through CTI with Kristen Rademacher completing the training and certification a few years later. Inspired by CTI training, CTI certification and the first edition of the book *Co-Active Coaching* (Whitworth et al., 1998), Theresa and Kristen further adapted and applied coaching principles and methods to working with students with ADHD and/or learning differences at the UNC-Chapel Hill Learning Center. The development, adoption, and expansion of ADHD/LD coaching reflected an increasing emphasis on more empowering, strengths-based methods of student support.

Studies on ADHD/LD coaching expanded in the first two decades of the 2000s. Empirical research found positive connections between ADHD/LD coaching for college students and goal attainment (Parker & Boutelle, 2009), executive functioning and self-regulation (Field et al., 2013; Parker et al., 2011; Richman et al., 2014; Swartz et al., 2005), study strategies, self-esteem, and

13

school satisfaction (Prevatt & Yelland, 2015), grade point average (DuPaul et al., 2017), and self-confidence and motivation (Bellman et al., 2015).

As academic coaching became increasingly popular for students with ADHD/LD at UNC-Chapel Hill, a university reorganization presented an opportunity to expand these services. By the 2010s, under the leadership of Dr. Kim Abels, Director of the Writing and Learning Center, who saw the alignment of academic coaching with writing center pedagogy (Lunsford, 1991; North, 1984), UNC-Chapel Hill began offering academic coaching to all undergraduates. Also, through Dr. Abel's leadership as well as support from the Finish Line Project at UNC-Chapel Hill (Babcock, 2015), Kristen Rademacher, Dr. Theresa Maitland, and Dr. Marc Howlett began offering campus coaching trainings to hundreds of faculty and staff, advancing efforts to create a university-wide culture of coaching. The Writing and Learning Center also conducts research on academic coaching, including a recent study that examined the effects of academic coaching on a broad cross-section of undergraduate students and found positive impacts on students' metacognitive awareness (Howlett, McWilliams, Rademacher, O'Neill, et al., 2021).

The empirical research literature on academic coaching in higher education has historically been less developed and cohesive than that for ADHD/LD coaching, although that is changing rapidly. A recent flurry of published studies has found positive connections between college academic coaching and goal attainment (Losch et al., 2016), the GPA of academically at-risk students (Capstick et al., 2019; Singhani et al., 2022; Vanacore & Dahan, 2021), student persistence and retention (Alzen et al., 2021), and credit-hour completion for community college students (Pechac & Slantcheva-Durst, 2021). Other empirical studies have investigated the impacts of an academic coaching training program on university faculty and staff (Howlett, McWilliams, Rademacher, Maitland, et al., 2021), expectations of students participating in peer academic coaching (Grabsch et al., 2021), and the relationship between peer academic coaching and motivational interviewing (MI) (Warner et al., 2018). Academic coaching seems to be generating increased interest from the global research community as evidenced by recent studies of text mining analyses of academic coaching intake reports in Korea (Lee et al., 2022) and student experiences with academic coaching in Norway (Saethern et al., 2022).

Although much more empirical and theoretical work needs to be done on academic coaching because differences in service provision make comparisons between studies difficult, our students attest to its effectiveness by choosing to utilize academic coaching on a day-in, day-out basis. At our university with over 18,000 undergraduates, academic coaching is voluntary. No one comes to our academic coaching appointments unless they take the effort to schedule one and show up. And thousands do each year. By the time they graduate, nearly 15% of all UNC-Chapel Hill students will have voluntarily participated in academic coaching at the Writing and Learning Center. Not only do thousands of students use academic coaching every year, a majority return for ongoing coaching.

Academic coaching in higher education, of course, is not limited to the work at UNC-Chapel Hill. A 2015 study found that over 100 colleges in the United States had active academic coaching programs (Robinson, 2015). Universities seem to be creating or expanding academic coaching services on a regular basis. The growth and development of academic coaching over the last two decades occurred within broader trends in higher education.

CONCURRENT DEVELOPMENTS

Our history of academic coaching at UNC-Chapel Hill occurred semi-autonomously within a larger transformation in university learning and teaching. In academic support, a transition was happening in moving from deficits-based to strengths-based approaches of working with students (Arendale, 2004, 2010). The more traditional deficit-based approaches are familiar in their focus on remedial services aimed at fixing students.

While many factors contributed to these shifts and expansions in university learning, one undergirding component was that a growing body of scholarly literature emphasized that positive interactions between undergraduate students and university faculty and staff were linked with student satisfaction, improved academic performance, persistence, graduation rates, and use of university resources (Cotten & Wilson, 2006; Demetriou & Schmitz-Sciborski, 2011; Kuh et al., 2006; Schreiner et al., 2011; Tinto, 2006). Empirical studies and on-the-ground experiences suggested that the quality of these interactions helps form the foundation of a supportive environment conducive to student engagement and success.

In the following sections, we briefly outline some of the theories, conceptual frameworks, and practices that inform and inspire academic coaching. Life and personal coaching were instrumental to the development of academic coaching, but they were already detailed earlier in this chapter. Each of the following sections only begins to touch on the connections between these developments and academic coaching, and we encourage you to refer to the chapter's references for more in-depth information. There are also theories and works not covered in these sections. For example, there are academic coaching programs and professionals that draw direct connections from positive psychology to their work (Ben-Yehuda, 2015; Robinson, 2015, p. 80; Seligman, 2007). And many university academic support programs are influenced by work on the zones of proximal development (Vygotsky, 1978) as well as the social construction of knowledge (Baxter Magolda, 2001; Bruffee, 1984; Ede, 1989). What we focus on in the following sections are where our own professional journeys helped connect theoretical frameworks and professional practices with academic coaching. For us as professional college academic coaches, here's what has helped inspire our work.

15

Self-Determination

Self-determination shares a similar trajectory to academic coaching within higher education. Self-determination emerged from the disability field and subsequently expanded in application to a wide range of college students (Field et al., 2003; Field & Parker, 2016). Self-determination theory emphasizes the importance of intrinsic motivation, a person doing something because they value it, to high-quality learning (Ryan & Deci, 2000). Self-determination is "the capacity to choose and to have those choices be the determinants of one's actions" (Deci & Ryan, 1985, p. 38). When applied to a higher education setting, self-determination can help college students increase self-awareness and reflection, improve goal setting, and become more autonomous learners.

Earlier in this chapter, we outlined the history of postsecondary ADHD/LD coaching, and these practices are often informed by self-determination. Multiple studies have utilized self-determination as a theoretical basis for empirical investigations of ADHD coaching in higher education (Ahmann et al., 2018; Parker & Boutelle, 2009). Self-determination has also been used as an organizing foundation for examining academic coaching in higher education more broadly (Sepulveda, 2020; Sleeper-Triplett & Fabrey, 2016). Defining and achieving goals, developing autonomy, and taking a strength-based approach are all foundational elements of coaching.

We frequently say that coaching is about moving to action, and the "action model of self-determination" (Field & Hoffman, n.d., 1994) is complementary to academic coaching. The action model of self-determination is iterative and cyclical with four main phases moving from knowing and valuing yourself and your context, to planning, to taking action, and then to experiencing and learning from the outcomes of those actions. These components occur within the larger context of a person's environment. While there are many similarities with the action model of self-determination, academic coaching almost always occurs within an interpersonal and relational context and its focus is on college academics.

Self-Authorship

Emerging from a different area of higher education research and practice, often within the realm of student affairs, self-authorship shares many similarities with both self-determination and academic coaching. The centrality of student agency is an especially prominent linkage. Expanding on the work of Kegan (1994), self-authorship can be defined as "the ability to collect, interpret, and analyze information and reflect on one's own beliefs in order to form judgments" (Baxter Magolda, 1998, p. 143).

Higher education professionals can support the promotion of students' self-authorship. Baxter Magolda summarized that the promotion of self-authorship involves "respecting learners' experience, concerns, and capacity to learn, sharing authority with learners, building trust, and engaging in mutual construction of meaning with learners" (2001, p. 231). These core concepts are reflected in the academic coaching model's fundamental beliefs that learners are the experts on their lives and that coaching is collaborative (see Chapter 4).

Helping empower students to become the authors of their academic lives is one way of conceptualizing an overarching goal of academic coaching. Self-authorship is notable for many reasons, including its emphasis on meaning-making (Baxter Magolda, 2008). One parallel between self-authorship and academic coaching is the latter's emphasis on helping students discover and develop their own internally generated meanings in contrast to the imposition of or acquiescence to external constructions of meaning. The subtitle of this book is *Coaching College Students for Success*. The word success is rife with meaning. It can be easy to have a prescribed view of success based on things like GPA. However, within academic coaching we work with students to help them explore and define what success means to them and to encourage the idea that success can have many meanings from person to person. "What does success mean to you?" and "What would success for you look like in this situation?" are common academic coaching questions.

Motivational Interviewing

From the field of healthcare, MI became an increasingly common form of working with people with health conditions and in programs such as substance abuse and tobacco cessation. Forms of health coaching have become ways of supplementing and complementing more traditional forms of medical approaches such as psychotherapy (Spence & Grant, 2012). While MI has a much different history and development from life coaching, there are many similarities, and in recent years, the practices of academic coaching and wellness coaching have begun to converge and look more like each other.

MI is primarily focused on behavior change, often within healthcare settings. There are many parallels with academic coaching. Although academic coaching might not always necessitate behavior change, a student's action plan in many instances will involve doing something new or different. MI is also well known for its OARS model of skills, which is comprised of (asking) open-ended questions, affirming, reflecting, and summarizing (Miller & Rollnick, 2012). These skills share similarities with academic coaching, and an individual receiving professional development training in MI can help strengthen one's academic coaching skills and tools.

Connections between MI and academic coaching have, like many elements of academic coaching, been underexamined in the scholarly literature. However, one recent study explored and argued for the connections between MI and college peer coaching (Warner et al., 2018). Health and wellness coaching is increasingly popular and common at universities, and many of these programs are based on MI principles and practices (Gibbs & Larcus, 2015; Southard et al., 2018).

Student Centeredness

Over the past decades, higher education has become increasingly student-centered. Student centeredness can be considered as tenets that promote accountability, autonomy, mutual respect, and a reflexive approach to teaching and learning (O'Neill & McMullin, 2005; Taylor, 2013; Wright, 2011). The rise of student centeredness parallels a shift in professor–student relationships and interactions. While faculty had generally occupied a role of "sage on the stage" increasingly there became efforts to adopt a role more akin to "guide on the side." Student-centered teaching and learning has also been cited as one of the hallmarks of inclusive instruction (Addy et al., 2021).

One way of thinking about student centeredness is the notion of "meeting students where they are." This concept helps illuminate that we as higher education professionals can tailor our approaches to an individual student and be more adaptive to them. The more traditional approach is having students arrive to college and sink or swim. The classic line from the initial convocation is "Look to your left. Look to your right. One of you won't be here at graduation."

While many college professionals believe in the effectiveness of student-centered learning, sometimes it can be challenging to translate these beliefs into day-to-day work. We maintain that academic coaching provides a method for operationalizing and implementing the ideas and principles of student-centered higher education. And academic support programs like academic coaching have been cited as models of student-centered learning on college campuses (Revuluri, 2021). As we'll explore in the coming chapters, academic coaching is about helping students decide for themselves what they want to do in terms of their academic goals and how they want to approach them.

Growth Mindset

The concept of the growth mindset has become pervasive in education. Most commonly associated with the work of Stanford psychologist Carol Dweck, a growth mindset can be defined as "the belief that abilities can be cultivated" (Dweck, 2006, p. 50). The growth mindset directly contrasts with a fixed mindset, which is the belief that talents, capabilities, and potential for achievement are essentially set. In working with college students, we hear evidence of a fixed mindset regularly. Students say things like, "I'm not a writer" or "I can't do math" or "I'm always late." These statements are often followed up with something akin to, "It's just who I am."

The concept of a growth mindset resonated within higher education as it promoted a positive approach based on potential and growth. Aiming to shift from a fixed to growth mindset proved important with higher education becoming increasingly diverse. Educators saw the growth mindset as a way of countering traditional structures and roles, and the growth mindset became a centerpiece of programs geared toward increasing the participation of historically underrepresented students in fields like STEM and medicine. Faculty having a growth mindset about the students they teach is an important element of creating inclusive classrooms (Hogan & Sathy, 2022; Sathy & Hogan, 2019).

To be an effective academic coach, we maintain you must believe the student you are working with is capable of learning and growth. We also believe that an academic coaching approach helps support the development of a student's growth mindset even if they may feel stuck or fixed at times. Academic coaching focuses on what students can do or can grow to do. We embrace challenges and, as we'll see in Chapter 4, that within the academic coaching framework we see challenges as opportunities for growth.

Appreciative Advising

In academic advising offices, professionals looking for more effective ways to work with students applied theories and practices from appreciative inquiry to create what became known as appreciative advising (Bloom et al., 2008, 2014; He & Hutson, 2016). Many of the core tenets and practices of appreciative advising, such as a strengths-based, student-centered approach and the emphasis on asking open-ended questions, parallel academic coaching.

The stages of appreciative advising share similarities with academic coaching (Bradley & Reynolds, 2021). Here are the six phases of appreciative advising (Bloom et al., 2008, p. 34):

- Disarm
- Discover
- Dream
- Design
- Deliver
- Don't settle

The strengths-based, collaborative, and student-centered nature of appreciative advising generated substantial interest within college academic and student support. Principles of appreciative advising have been used to structure first-year experience courses (Hutson, 2010). There have been calls to incorporate appreciative advising into college learning centers (Truschel, 2008). The Association for the Coaching and Tutoring Profession (ACPT), which offers certification in academic coaching, has a module dedicated to "Appreciative Coaching," which includes covering the six phases of appreciative advising described above (Association for the Coaching and Tutoring Profession, n.d.). A nationwide survey of academic coaching programs found that while few universities relied upon established theoretical or conceptual frameworks, for those that did specify a theoretical or conceptual framework that appreciative advising/inquiry was most common (Robinson, 2015, p. 79).

Self-Regulated Learning and Metacognition

Of the many theoretical foundations for academic coaching, it is perhaps self-regulated learning (SRL) that aligns most closely. SRL is the process by which students are active participants in their learning (Greene, 2018; Schunk & Greene, 2018; Zimmerman, 2013). SRL can be defined as "the process whereby learners personally activate and sustain cognitions, affects, and behaviors that are systemically oriented toward the attainment of personal goals" (Zimmerman & Schunk, 2011, p. 1). Zimmerman further defines SRL as "proactive processes that students use to acquire academic skill, such as setting goals, selecting and deploying strategies, and self-monitoring one's effectiveness, rather than as a reactive event that happens to students due to impersonal forces" (2013, pp. 166–167).

Academic self-regulation is comprised of six main areas (Seli & Dembo, 2020; Zimmerman & Risemberg, 1997):

- Motivation
- Methods of learning
- Use of time
- Physical environment
- Social environment
- Monitoring performance

Metacognition, which is a key element of SRL, has received widespread attention for its utility in helping students learn (McGuire & McGuire, 2015). Metacognition is often defined as "thinking about thinking," and within academic self-regulation, it is the process by which monitoring performance occurs. When academic coaches talk about and work with students on becoming more active learners, we must include metacognition. Metacognition is critical to SRL because if students are not monitoring the different elements of academic self-regulation ("I've been working on the same problem for two hours") then it's much harder to consciously regulate their actions ("I'm taking a break to walk around the building and then start outlining a research paper. I'll go to office hours tomorrow to ask about this problem"). Studying, which sometimes is a nebulous term, can be understood and examined through the framework of SRL (Winne & Hadwin, 1998).

We believe that academic coaching provides targeted support to help students develop their SRL and metacognition. While more work is warranted in this area, multiple authors have connected academic coaching with SRL (Barkley, 2011; Howlett et al., 2019; Howlett, McWilliams, Rademacher, O'Neill, et al., 2021; Mitchell & Gansemer-Topf, 2016; Reynolds, 2020). Academic coaching sessions frequently facilitate student engagement with the six main components of academic self-regulation listed above through a structured, interpersonal conversation centered on open-ended questions. Open-ended academic coaching questions are described in detail in Chapter 5 and discussed throughout the book. We ask students questions like:

- "How do you decide where to start when you begin studying?"
- "Where do you do your best writing?"
- "What's your evaluation of this strategy?"
- "How do you approach the readings for this class?"
- "What are signs that your studying has become less effective?"
- "What do you think will help you improve?"

The processes of SRL are iterative and cyclical just like academic coaching. As students develop their SRL skills, they become more strategic, flexible, and self-directed in their learning.

A PATH FORWARD FOR STUDENT-CENTERED, STRENGTHS-BASED ACADEMIC SUPPORT

One of the challenges with concepts like student centeredness and growth mindset is that, while these beliefs and approaches are foundational to more empowering forms of student support, by themselves they often do not provide a method for going about that work. To put it another way, a person can believe students have an inherent ability to grow, learn, and improve, and they may want to take a student-centered approach. Yet, they may not know how to translate that wish to a method of working with students on a day-to-day basis. You can want to be more student-centered, but how do you do that?

We believe that using this book as the basis for providing academic coaching or applying elements of academic coaching will give you tangible methods, strategies, and frameworks to a holistic and strengths-based approach to working with college students. In the upcoming chapters, we'll cover the definition of academic coaching, the fundamental beliefs and assumptions, the tools and skills of academic coaching, how to structure a coaching conversation, and the application of academic coaching approaches to a wide variety of higher education contexts and student populations.

For higher education professionals, staff and faculty wanting to provide or incorporate academic coaching into their work, you are in the right place. Let's dive into that topic right now!

REFERENCES

Addy, T. M., Dube, D., Mitchell, K. A., & SoRelle, M. E. (2021). *What inclusive instructors do: Principles and practices for excellence in college teaching*. Stylus Publishing.

Ahmann, E., Tuttle, L. J., Saviet, M., & Wright, S. D. (2018). A descriptive review of ADHD coaching research: Implications for college students. *Journal of Postsecondary Education and Disability*, *31*(1), 17–39. https://eric.ed.gov/?id=EJ1182373

Alexander, G., & Renshaw, B. (2005). *Supercoaching: The missing ingredient for high performance*. Random House.

Alzen, J. L., Burkhardt, A., Diaz-Bilello, E., Elder, E., Sepulveda, A., Blankenheim, A., & Board, L. (2021). Academic coaching and its relationship to student performance, retention, and credit completion. *Innovative Higher Education*, *46*(5), 539–563. https://doi.org/10.1007/s10755-021-09554-w

Arendale, D. R. (2004). Mainstreamed academic assistance and enrichment for all students: The historical origins of learning assistance centers. *Research for Education Reform*. https://hdl.handle.net/11299/200364

Arendale, D. R. (2010). *Access at the crossroads: Learning assistance in higher education*. ASHE Higher Education Report.

Association for the Coaching and Tutoring Profession. (n.d.). *Association for the Coaching and Tutoring Profession: Academic coaching certification*. Retrieved May 25, 2022, from https://www.myactp.com/certifications-home/

Babcock, P. (2015, March). Reaching the finish line: $3 million grant to boost retention, graduation rates. *Carolina Arts & Sciences Magazine*. https://magazine.college.unc.edu/2015/03/finishline2/

Barkley, A. (2011). Academic coaching for enhanced learning. *NACTA Journal*, *55*(1), 76–81. https://www.jstor.org/stable/nactajournal.55.1.76

Baxter Magolda, M. B. (1998). Developing self-authorship in young adult life. *Journal of College Student Development*, *39*(2), 143–156.

Baxter Magolda, M. B. (2001). *Making their own way: Narratives for transforming higher education to promote self-development*. Stylus Publishing.

Baxter Magolda, M. B. (2008). Three elements of self-authorship. *Journal of College Student Development*, *49*(4), 269–284. https://doi.org/10.1353/csd.0.0016

Bellman, S., Burgstahler, S., & Hinke, P. (2015). Academic coaching: Outcomes from a pilot group of postsecondary STEM students with disabilities. *Journal of Postsecondary Education and Disability*, *28*(1), 103–108. https://files.eric.ed.gov/fulltext/EJ1066319.pdf

Ben-Yehuda, M. (2015). The route to success—Personal-academic coaching program. *Procedia-Social and Behavioral Sciences*, *209*, 323–328. https://doi.org/10.1016/j.sbspro.2015.11.242

Bettinger, E. P., & Baker, R. B. (2014). The effects of student coaching: An evaluation of a randomized experiment in student advising. *Educational Evaluation and Policy Analysis*, *36*(1), 3–19. https://doi.org/10.3102/0162373713500523

Bloom, J. L., Hutson, B. L., & He, Y. (2008). *The appreciative advising revolution*. Stipes Publishing.

Bloom, J. L., Hutson, B. L., He, Y., & Konkle, E. (2014). *The appreciative advising revolution training workbook: Translating theory to practice*. Stipes Publishing L.L.C.

Bradley, J., & Reynolds, M. (2021). Appreciative academic coaching. *Journal of Appreciative Education*, *7*(1), 15–21.

Bruffee, K. A. (1984). Collaborative learning and the "conversation of mankind." *College English*, *46*(7), 635–652. https://doi.org/10.2307/376924

Byron, J., & Parker, D. R. (2002). College students with ADHD: New challenges and directions. In L. C. Brinckerhoff, J. M. McGuire, & S. F. Shaw (Eds.), *Postsecondary education and transition for students with learning disabilities* (2nd ed., pp. 335–387). PRO-ED, Inc.

Capstick, M. K., Harrell-Williams, L. M., Cockrum, C. D., & West, S. L. (2019). Exploring the effectiveness of academic coaching for academically at-risk college students. *Innovative Higher Education*, *44*(3), 219–231. https://doi.org/10.1007/s10755-019-9459-1

Co-Active Training Institute. (n.d.). *Our story*. Retrieved May 26, 2022, from https://coactive.com/about/our-story/#history

Cotten, S. R., & Wilson, B. (2006). Student–faculty interactions: Dynamics and determinants. *Higher Education*, *51*(4), 487–519. https://doi.org/10.1007/s10734-004-1705-4

Deci, E. L., & Ryan, R. M. (1985). *Intrinsic motivation and self-determination in human behavior*. Plenum Press.

Demetriou, C., & Schmitz-Sciborski, A. (2011). Integration, motivation, strengths and optimism: Retention theories past, present and future. In *Proceedings of the 7th national symposium on student retention* (p. 201).

DuPaul, G. J., Dahlstrom-Hakki, I., Gormley, M. J., Fu, Q., Pinho, T. D., & Banerjee, M. (2017). College students with ADHD and LD: Effects of support services on academic performance. *Learning Disabilities Research & Practice*, *32*(4), 246–256. https://doi.org/10.1111/ldrp.12143

Dweck, C. S. (2006). *Mindset: The new psychology of success*. Ballantine Books.

23

Ede, L. (1989). Writing as a social process: A theoretical foundation for writing centers? *The Writing Center Journal*, *9*(2), 3–13. https://www.jstor.org/stable/43444122

Farrell, E. F. (2007, July 20). Some colleges provide success coaches for students. *The Chronicle of Higher Education*, 44–47.

Field, S., & Hoffman, A. (n.d.). *An action model for self-determination.* 2BSD: To Be Self-Determined. Retrieved May 18, 2022, from https://www.beselfdetermined.com/model/

Field, S., & Hoffman, A. (1994). Development of a model for self-determination. *Career Development for Exceptional Individuals*, *17*(2), 159–169.

Field, S., & Parker, D. (2016). *Becoming self-determined: Creating thoughtful learners in a standards-driven, admissions-frenzied culture.* Association on Higher Education and Disability.

Field, S., Parker, D. R., Sawilowsky, S., & Rolands, L. (2013). Assessing the impact of ADHD coaching services on university students' learning skills, self-regulation, and well-being. *Journal of Postsecondary Education and Disability*, *26*(1), 67–81. https://files.eric.ed.gov/fulltext/EJ1026813.pdf

Field, S., Sarver, M. D., & Shaw, S. F. (2003). Self-determination: A key to success in postsecondary education for students with learning disabilities. *Remedial and Special Education*, *24*(6), 339–349. https://doi.org/10.1177%2F07419325030240060501

Gibbs, T., & Larcus, J. (2015). Wellness coaching: Helping students thrive. *Journal of Student Affairs*, *24*(23), 23–34.

Grabsch, D. K., Peña, R. A., & Parks, K. J. (2021). Expectations of students participating in voluntary peer academic coaching. *Journal of College Reading and Learning*, *51*(2), 95–109. https://doi.org/10.1080/10790195.2020.1798827

Greene, J. A. (2018). *Self-regulation in education.* Routledge.

He, Y., & Hutson, B. (2016). Appreciative assessment in academic advising. *The Review of Higher Education*, *39*(2), 213–240. https://doi.org/10.1353/rhe.2016.0003

Hogan, K. A., & Sathy, V. (2022). *Inclusive teaching: Strategies for promoting equity in the college classroom.* West Virginia University Press.

Howlett, M. A., McWilliams, M. A., O'Neill, J. C., Rademacher, K., Maitland, T. L., Abels, K., Demetriou, C., & Panter, A. T. (2019). *Academic coaching: Assessing a higher education intervention within a self-regulated learning framework.* American Educational Research Association, Toronto, Canada.

Howlett, M. A., McWilliams, M. A., Rademacher, K., Maitland, T. L., O'Neill, J. C., Abels, K., Demetriou, C., & Panter, A. (2021). An academic coaching training program for university professionals: A mixed methods examination. *Journal of Student Affairs Research and Practice*, *58*(3), 335–349. https://doi.org/10.1080/19496591.2020.1784750

Howlett, M. A., McWilliams, M. A., Rademacher, K., O'Neill, J. C., Maitland, T. L., Abels, K., Demetriou, C., & Panter, A. T. (2021). Investigating the effects of academic coaching on college students' metacognition. *Innovative Higher Education*, *46*(2), 189–204. https://doi.org/10.1007/s10755-020-09533-7

Hutson, B. L. (2010). The impact of an appreciative advising-based university studies course on college student first-year experience. *Journal of Applied Research in Higher Education*, *2*(1), 4–13. https://doi.org/10.1108/17581184201000001

International Coaching Federation. (n.d.-a). *History of ICF*. International Coaching Federation. Retrieved May 26, 2022, from https://coachingfederation.org/history

International Coaching Federation. (n.d.-b). *Learn the facts about coaching*. Retrieved March 7, 2022, from https://experiencecoaching.com/learn/

Kegan, R. (1994). *In over our heads: The mental demands of modern life*. Harvard University Press.

Kuh, G. D., Kinzie, J. L., Buckley, J. A., Bridges, B. K., & Hayek, J. C. (2006). *What matters to student success: A review of the literature* (Vol. 8). National Postsecondary Education Cooperative, Washington, DC.

Lee, A., Lee, S. J., Lee, J. Y., & Rhee, E. (2022). Text mining analysis of Korean university students' academic coaching intake session reports. *International Journal of Environmental Research and Public Health*, *19*(10), 6208. https://doi.org/10.3390/ijerph19106208

Losch, S., Traut-Mattausch, E., Mühlberger, M. D., & Jonas, E. (2016). Comparing the effectiveness of individual coaching, self-coaching, and group training: How leadership makes the difference. *Frontiers in Psychology*, *7*, 629. https://doi.org/10.3389/fpsyg.2016.00629

Lunsford, A. (1991). Collaboration, control, and the idea of a writing center. *The Writing Center Journal*, *12*(1), 3–10. https://www.jstor.org/stable/43441887

McGuire, S. Y., & McGuire, S. (2015). *Teach students how to learn: Strategies you can incorporate into any course to improve student metacognition, study skills, and motivation*. Stylus Publishing.

Miller, W. R., & Rollnick, S. (2012). *Motivational interviewing: Helping people change* (3rd ed.). Guilford press.

Mitchell, J. J., & Gansemer-Topf, A. M. (2016). Academic coaching and self-regulation: Promoting the success of students with disabilities. *Journal of Postsecondary Education and Disability*, *29*(3), 249–256. http://files.eric.ed.gov/fulltext/EJ1123788.pdf

North, S. M. (1984). The idea of a writing center. *College English*, *46*(5), 433–446. https://doi.org/10.2307/377047

O'Connor, J., & Lages, A. (2007). *How coaching works: The essential guide to the history and practice of effective coaching*. A & C Black Publishers Ltd.

O'Neill, G., & McMullin, B. (2005). Student-centered learning: What does it mean for students and lecturers? In G. O'Neill, S. Moore, & B. McMullin (Eds.), *Emerging issues in the practice of university learning and teaching* (pp. 27–36). AISHE.

Parker, D. R., & Boutelle, K. (2009). Executive function coaching for college students with learning disabilities and ADHD: A new approach for fostering self-determination. *Learning Disabilities Research & Practice, 24*(4), 204–215. https://doi.org/10.1111/j.1540-5826.2009.00294.x

Parker, D. R., & Byron, J. (1998). Differences between college students with LD and AD/HD: Practical implications for service providers. In P. O. Quinn & A. McCormick (Eds.), *Re-thinking AD/HD: A guide to fostering success in students with AD/HD at the college level* (pp. 14–30). Advantage Books.

Parker, D. R., Hoffman, S. F., Sawilowsky, S., & Rolands, L. (2011). An examination of the effects of ADHD coaching on university students' executive functioning. *Journal of Postsecondary Education and Disability, 24*(2), 115–132. https://files.eric.ed.gov/fulltext/EJ943698.pdf

Pechac, S., & Slantcheva-Durst, S. (2021). Coaching toward completion: Academic coaching factors influencing community college student success. *Journal of College Student Retention: Research, Theory & Practice, 23*(3), 722–746. https://doi.org/10.1177/1521025119869849

Prevatt, F., & Yelland, S. (2015). An empirical evaluation of ADHD coaching in college students. *Journal of Attention Disorders, 19*(8), 666–677. https://doi.org/10.1177/1087054713480036

Quinn, P. O., Ratey, N., & Maitland, T. L. (2000). *Coaching college students with AD/HD: Issues and answers.* Advantage Books.

Revuluri, S. (2021). Student-centered learning and teaching—Lessons from academic support. In S. Hoidn & M. Klemencic (Eds.), *The Routledge International handbook of student-centered learning and teaching in higher education* (pp. 414–423). Routledge.

Reynolds, A. K. (2020). Academic coaching for learners in medical education: Twelve tips for the learning specialist. *Medical Teacher, 42*(6), 616–621. https://doi.org/10.1080/0142159X.2019.1607271

Richman, E. L., Rademacher, K. N., & Maitland, T. L. (2014). Coaching and college success. *Journal of Postsecondary Education and Disability, 27*(1), 33–50. https://files.eric.ed.gov/fulltext/EJ1029647.pdf

Robinson, C. E. (2015). *Academic/success coaching: A description of an emerging field in higher education* [PhD Thesis]. University of South Carolina.

Ryan, R. M., & Deci, E. L. (2000). Intrinsic and extrinsic motivations: Classic definitions and new directions. *Contemporary Educational Psychology, 25*(1), 54–67. https://doi.org/10.1006/ceps.1999.1020

Saethern, B. B., Glømmen, A. M., Lugo, R., & Ellingsen, P. (2022). Students' experiences of academic coaching in Norway: A pilot study. *International Journal of Mentoring and Coaching in Education*, ahead-of-print. https://doi.org/10.1108/IJMCE-07-2021-0077

Sathy, V., & Hogan, K. (2019, July 22). How to make your teaching more inclusive. *Chronicle of Higher Education.* https://www.chronicle.com/article/how-to-make-your-teaching-more-inclusive/

Schreiner, L. A., Noel, P., Anderson, E., & Cantwell, L. (2011). The impact of faculty and staff on high-risk college student persistence. *Journal of College Student Development*, *52*(3), 321–338. https://doi.org/10.1353/csd.2011.0044

Schunk, D. H., & Greene, J. A. (2018). Historical, contemporary, and future perspectives on self-regulated learning and performance. In D. H. Schunk & J. A. Greene (Eds.), *Handbook of self-regulation of learning and performance* (pp. 1–15). Taylor & Francis.

Seli, H., & Dembo, M. H. (2020). *Motivation and learning strategies for college success: A focus on self-regulated learning* (6th ed.). Routledge.

Seligman, M. E. (2007). Coaching and positive psychology. *Australian Psychologist*, *42*(4), 266–267. https://doi.org/10.1080/00050060701648233

Sepulveda, A. (2020). *Coaching college students to thrive: Exploring coaching practices in higher education* [PhD Thesis, University of Northern Colorado]. https://www.proquest.com/docview/2424513317

Singhani, S., McLaren-Poole, K., & Bernier, R. A. (2022). Evaluating the effectiveness of academic coaching for college students. *Learning Assistance Review (TLAR)*, *27*(1), 219–250.

Sleeper-Triplett, J., & Fabrey, C. (2016). Academic coaching: Using a coach approach to build student self-determination. In S. Field & D. Parker (Eds.), *Becoming self-determined: Creating thoughtful learners in a standards-driven, admissions-frenzied culture* (pp. 87–113). Association on Higher Education and Disability.

Southard, K. J., Welk, G. J., Lansing, J. E., Perez, M., & Ellingson, L. D. (2018). Peer health coach training practicum: Evidence from a flipped classroom. *CIRTL Reports*, *12*. https://lib.dr.iastate.edu/cirtl_reports/12

Spence, G. B., & Grant, A. M. (2007). Professional and peer life coaching and the enhancement of goal striving and well-being: An exploratory study. *The Journal of Positive Psychology*, *2*(3), 185–194. https://doi.org/10.1080/17439760701228896

Spence, G. B., & Grant, A. M. (2012). Coaching and well-being: A brief review of existing evidence, relevant theory and implications for practitioners. In S. David, I. Boniwell, & A. Conley Ayers (Eds.), *The Oxford handbook of happiness*. Oxford University Press. https://doi.org/10.1093/oxfordhb/9780199557257.013.0075

Sussman, S. (2000). AD/HD coaching: Looking back and looking ahead. In P. O. Quinn, N. Ratey, & T. L. Maitland (Eds.), *Coaching college students with AD/HD: Issues and answers*. Advantage Books.

Swartz, S. L., Prevatt, F., & Proctor, B. E. (2005). A coaching intervention for college students with attention deficit/hyperactivity disorder. *Psychology in the Schools*, *42*(6), 647–656. https://doi.org/10.1002/pits.20101

Taylor, J. (2013). What is student centredness and is it enough? *International Journal of the First Year in Higher Education*, *4*(2), 39–48. https://doi.org/10.5204/intjfyhe.v4i1.168

Tinto, V. (2006). Research and practice of student retention: What next? *Journal of College Student Retention: Research, Theory & Practice*, *8*(1), 1–19. https://doi.org/10.2190/4YNU-4TMB-22DJ-AN4W

Truschel, J. (2008). Does the use of appreciative advising work? *The Learning Assistance Review, 13*(2), 7–16.

Vanacore, S. M., & Dahan, T. A. (2021). Assessing the effectiveness of a coaching intervention for students on academic probation. *Journal of College Reading and Learning, 51*(1), 3–16. https://doi.org/10.1080/10790195.2019.1684855

Vygotsky, L. S. (1978). *Mind in society: The development of higher psychological processes* (M. Cole, Ed.). Harvard University Press.

Warner, Z., Neater, W., Clark, L., & Lee, J. (2018). Peer coaching and motivational interviewing in postsecondary settings: Connecting retention theory with practice. *Journal of College Reading and Learning, 48*(3), 159–174. https://doi.org/10.1080/10790195.2018.1472940

Whitmore, J. (2017). *Coaching for performance: The principles and practice of coaching and leadership* (5th ed.). Nicholas Brealey Publishing.

Whitworth, L., Kimsey-House, H., & Sandahl, P. (1998). *Co-Active Coaching: New skills for coaching people toward success in work and life*. Nicholas Brealey Publishing.

Winne, P. H., & Hadwin, A. E. (1998). Studying as self-regulated learning. In D. J. Hacker, J. Dunlosky, & A. C. Graesser (Eds.), *Metacognition in educational theory and practice* (pp. 277–304). Routledge.

Wright, G. B. (2011). Student-centered learning in higher education. *International Journal of Teaching and Learning in Higher Education, 23*(3), 92–97.

Zimmerman, B. J. (2013). From cognitive modeling to self-regulation: A social cognitive career path. *Educational Psychologist, 48*(3), 135–147. https://doi.org/10.1080/00461520.2013.794676

Zimmerman, B. J., & Risemberg, R. (1997). Self-regulatory dimensions of academic learning and motivation. In G. D. Phye (Ed.), *Handbook of academic learning: Construction of knowledge* (pp. 105–125). Academic Press.

Zimmerman, B. J., & Schunk, D. H. (Eds.). (2011). *Handbook of self-regulation of learning and performance*. Routledge.

Zwart, L. M., & Kallemeyn, L. M. (2001). Peer-based coaching for college students with ADHD and learning disabilities. *Journal of Postsecondary Education and Disability, 15*(1), 1–15.

Part II

Academic Coaching Model

Chapter 3

Definition

As examined in the previous chapter, academic coaching entered colleges and universities as a natural progression from professional and personal coaching as educators began reconsidering best practices for instruction and academic support.

So, what exactly is academic coaching, and what do academic coaches do?

The model of academic coaching detailed in this book was inspired by the training and certification we received from the Co-Active® Training Institute (CTI). There was plenty to like about their coaching philosophy: the focus on collaboration, inquiry and curiosity, and the belief that coaches help clients reflect and grow. But our clients were college students, steeped in academia. They were transitioning to adulthood, adjusting to the rigor of college-level courses, exploring interests, forming identities, and building skills to manage their time and themselves in largely unstructured environments.

Before embracing a coach approach with students, we'd often provide direct instruction in individual academic counseling sessions. Students would present an issue ("I failed my chemistry test," "I procrastinate too much," or "I can't keep up with the reading"), and we'd offer solutions ("Ask your instructor for help," "Use a calendar," or "Make a reading schedule"). Most students were agreeable to our direction with few questions.

After deciding to embrace coaching principles and their application to college academic support, we shifted away from a didactic, hierarchical model of working with students in which we diagnosed a problem and prescribed a solution. Instead, we wanted to facilitate students' long-term growth and development of skills through collaborative, action-oriented conversations. We wanted our students to take a more active role in their coaching sessions with us, and we wanted to align our approaches with *their* strengths, interests, and goals. Also, we wanted our methods to reflect the belief that students could cultivate the agency and tools to change their academic outcomes.

The definition of academic coaching we came to adopt is based on many of the theoretical frameworks and developments in higher education outlined in the previous chapter along with the impactful training and certification we received from CTI (Kimsey-House et al., 2018). We acknowledge that there are other approaches and conceptualizations of academic coaching. This is not the only model of academic coaching, and that's perfectly okay. But after decades of professional work, research, and reflection, here's our definition of academic coaching:

Academic coaching is a collaborative and trusting relationship where through structured conversations, students are empowered to:

1. Set and take action toward goals
2. Stay accountable and committed to goals
3. Understand their habits and thinking patterns
4. Understand their strengths and weaknesses
5. Improve self-regulation of learning, behaviors, and emotions
6. Learn effective study strategies

Let's unpack the first part of the definition.

ACADEMIC COACHING IS A COLLABORATIVE AND TRUSTING RELATIONSHIP

A collaborative relationship means it is not hierarchical. Yes, academic coaches are professionals with expertise. And yes, students seek coaches because they need help, or because they want to change or improve an aspect of their academic life. But the aim of a coach is to facilitate students' growth, not to simply provide advice, direction, or to impart their knowledge (as examples of what academic coaching is not). We want the student to be in the proverbial driver's seat of the coaching relationship, with the coach riding along as an active passenger. That means the student has their hands on the wheel, but the coach might be reading the map, noting oncoming traffic, or ensuring they are heading in the direction the student wants. In this analogy of academic coaching, neither the student nor the coach can be passive.

Let's say a student comes to an academic coaching session seeking assistance with time management because they aren't sleeping enough and arrive late to morning classes. A non-collaborative session might have the coach simply tell the student to make an agreement with their roommate to get to bed by midnight. Similarly, a less-collaborative session might have the coach patiently wait for the student to generate some ideas on their own without providing any input because after all, academic coaching is where students develop problem-solving agency. Collaborative coaching, however, means both the student and the coach are putting their heads together to figure out a creative and suitable plan to adjust the student's sleep routine.

There are many life scenarios where collaboration is not only unhelpful but also inappropriate. A surgical team likely doesn't need or want the family of their patient joining them in the operating room to offer advice or cheer them on. But collaboration is a key element of academic coaching.

The collaborative design of the coaching relationship also implies that the coach values and needs the student's input. Academic coaches cultivate productive relationships with students when they recognize—and remind their students—that the students know themselves better than anyone. Students certainly know themselves better than their academic coach! Students' past and current experiences in and out of the classroom hold great significance in a coaching session. Students don't arrive to a first coaching session as blank slates, as if they are newly awakened to their role as students. They've been students for most of their lives. They have accrued innumerable strategies and techniques in their experiences as learners, some helpful and some perhaps in need of refinement. Regardless, academic coaches want to know about these strategies as they can provide a launching off point in the coaching conversation. Without student input, academic coaching is not actually coaching at all.

The coach and the student are partners in the coaching relationship, combining the coaches' understanding of learning theories and best practices with the students' understanding of themselves and what they want from the session.

A successful academic coaching relationship is fueled by trust. Students need to trust that their coach will provide a safe, accepting space for honest reflection. Students need to trust that their coach will not judge them for whatever they bring to the conversation: successes, failures, struggles, questions, worries, dreams, and so on. Depending on the student and the circumstances, a degree of vulnerability and candor can be helpful in establishing an ultimately fruitful coaching relationship. But without trusting their coach, students will likely be reluctant to engage in an open and authentic conversation. And without authenticity from the student, the benefits of academic coaching will be limited.

Another critical component in building trust is respect, and students need to know that they have the respect of their academic coach. This means that their coach will give them their undivided attention during a session, they won't dismiss or minimize a student's concern, and they will hold whatever comes up in the conversation with the utmost importance and care.

Students also need to trust that their academic coach has no hidden agenda. Academic coaches work with students through a holistic lens and meet them at their point of need. In this model, there is no "academic coaching curriculum" where coaches lead students through a sequenced set of skills that they believe they need. Trust is damaged when a coach disregards where students are on their academic journey, and instead tries to tell them where they think they ought to be. Picture a student telling their coach that they'd like to get a handle on their all-consuming astronomy class, but the coach thinks the student should prioritize their efforts to their journalism course, which is a course within their major. The coach might be well intentioned with a decent point—and there's a coaching skill we'll review in Chapter 7 where coaches can float suggestions to the student. But dismissing the student's expressed interest to focus on their astronomy class can come across as paternalistic and can leave the student feeling frustrated. Trust does not grow in this sort of environment, so it's important for the agenda of the coaching conversation to be the student's, not the coach's.

Before we go further, we want to assure you that we are not suggesting you toss your professional expertise out the window during coaching conversations with students. Your experience and knowledge about your institution compared to a student's can provide valuable insights and facts. There are many times when it is appropriate and important for you to share your point of view with a student. The way you share, however, can make a difference in strengthening the student's trust in you or weakening it.

One final word about trust. In situations where seeking academic coaching is voluntary, the trust between the student and the coach is likely strengthened. Voluntary coaching keeps the students in the driver's seat which might mitigate any defensiveness they might feel. We do understand, however, that in many organizations, students might be required to see an academic coach for numerous reasons. Perhaps it's a step in getting off academic probation; maybe receiving academic support is built into the first-year experience or into the daily life of a student-athlete. When this is the case, the academic coach must demonstrate to the student that they want to make the session as valuable as possible for them.

Now that we examined the first part of the definition—academic coaching is a collaborative and trusting relationship—let's continue to the next part.

ACADEMIC COACHING IS A STRUCTURED CONVERSATION

The heart of academic coaching is the fact that it's a conversation. But it's not the sort of conversation one might have with a friend, though effective coaches are friendly. And it's not the type of conversation one might have with a mentor or a consultant, because coaches aren't necessarily sharing their expertise or experiences with students. Neither is it a conversation one might have with a counselor or therapist who may assist clients in wrestling with an array of mental health concerns.

An academic coaching conversation is highly structured. As you will see in Chapter 6, both the academic coach and student play active and specific roles. Coaches guide students through distinct phases of the conversation, with clear starting and ending points. Conversations between an academic coach and a student can occur on an ongoing basis, or they can take place just once. Coaching conversations can run for an hour or as briefly as five or ten minutes.

The point to understand is that when an academic coach and a student come together, regardless of the length or frequency of sessions, they will engage in a deliberate discussion that follows a progression of steps. Ultimately, those steps lead to action that the student agrees to take.

COMPONENTS OF THE DEFINITION

And now, let's dig into the rest of the definition. Academic coaching empowers students to:

1. Set and take action toward goals
2. Stay accountable and committed to goals
3. Understand their habits and thinking patterns
4. Understand their strengths and weaknesses
5. Improve self-regulation of learning, behavior, and emotions
6. Learn effective study strategies

With collaboration and trust as the foundation of the coaching relationship, and with the structure of the conversation in place, the student and coach roll up their sleeves and get to work. Through academic coaching, students learn how to become goal-centered in large and small ways. As coaches, we want students to develop the habit of asking themselves what they want and need. For example, if a student has several hours of unstructured time between classes, we want them to consider how they'd like to use that time. If they have a midterm exam at the end of the week, we want them to consider a study plan. If a student hopes to secure a summer internship, we want them to consider the resources needed to discover what sort of internships they are interested in, and what the application process entails. By determining what they want or need for themselves on large and small scales, college students begin to articulate goals. And having goals creates purpose and drives behaviors (Locke, 1996; Locke & Latham, 1990, 2006; Pintrich, 2000; Schunk, 1989; Seli & Dembo, 2020). When a student, for example, sets a goal to avoid returning to their residence hall between classes where they often end up taking a nap and losing time, they can then imagine what they might do instead. Perhaps, they decide to use that time to go to the library and finish reading assignments for the next day, or perhaps they elect to visit the gym for a workout, or maybe they opt to plant themselves in a coffee shop or the student union to catch up on email. In some ways, what they choose to do between classes matters less than developing the practice of consciously setting a goal.

As students set large and small goals, we also want them to envision how to take action and stay committed to these goals. We help them turn their goals into a series of concrete steps (about which you'll read much more in coming chapters).

Equally important in designing a plan is designing ways to stay committed and accountable. What use is a plan without follow-through?! And what better way to ensure follow-through than some sort of accountability? Academic coaching trains students to think about how to stay committed to their goals and make them achievable. Let's say our student who intends to avoid naps in their residence hall between classes commits to going to the gym instead. Through the academic coaching conversation, they will consider how to optimize success for their goal. Maybe they need to set an alert on their phone as a reminder to pack gym clothes before heading to their first class, or maybe they'd be more likely to stick to the plan if they enlist a friend to join them, or maybe drafting a simple work-out plan would strengthen their motivation. Maybe they want to keep and share a record of their workouts with a friend and/or their academic coach as a form of accountability while building this new routine.

The point is, academic coaching assumes that while setting a goal is an important first step in creating purpose and shaping behaviors, it also assumes there is a critical need to think through how to transform the goal from an abstract idea to a specific, tangible plan.

Another key component of our academic coaching definition is the aim to strengthen students' understanding of themselves. Our academic coaching model is designed to encourage self-reflection. Students are given opportunities to examine their habits and thinking patterns in many aspects of their lives and to evaluate the merit of these habits. We encourage them to consider the habitual way they approach reading, take notes, use a calendar, prepare for essay exams, or handle disappointment. Then, we encourage them to think about how satisfied they are with the results. Does the way they take notes in class, for example, yield a useful record of the lecture that then aids their studying? If not, we coach students to recognize that they might want to explore another method. How about their habit of believing that one poor test grade is an indicator that they do not have the skills to succeed in that particular subject? How does that belief system impact their confidence and motivation to maintain effort or perhaps willingness to explore new ways of studying? If a student can recognize that their habit of putting full stock in one test grade can be limiting, we coach them to explore alternative attitudes.

Academic coaching can shine a light on students' habits, which allows students to view them more objectively and work toward changing these behaviors and thinking patterns if desired.

Understanding oneself includes knowing one's strengths and weaknesses. As mentioned above, self-reflection is a huge part of academic coaching, and students are given ample opportunities to analyze their academic successes and struggles. Sometimes students already have good awareness of their strengths or weaknesses. "My writing can be really clear and crisp once I have a solid thesis." "I'm good at decoding multiple choice questions and selecting the correct responses."

"I'm initially shy with people I don't know, so visiting my instructors in office hours can be hard." "My ADHD can make me impulsive, and without adequate preparation, I often make small errors on detail-oriented tests like math."

But sometimes students aren't sure how to address an area of weakness or perhaps even doubt they can change. Likewise, students might not know how to fully utilize their strengths. For example, imagine the student who is reticent to talk individually to their professor. They might generalize their reservation to initiate a meeting with a professor as, "I have always been shy and talking with new people will always be hard for me. That's just the way I am." Case closed, nothing to do about the situation. However, through academic coaching, a student can explore strategies to feel more comfortable with their professor, and more importantly see themselves as capable of growth. The student who recognizes their writing as clear and crisp can explore how to capitalize on this strength with their coach. In what other ways can their writing skills help them progress toward their goals?

In short, by better understanding their strengths and weaknesses, academic coaching can help students develop agency to expand upon their strengths and find supports for their weaknesses. Through practice, college students can actively improve their academic self-awareness (Nilson, 2013).

Self-regulation is a broad term that describes the process through which we learn and develop new skills and the process by which we regulate our learning, emotions, and behaviors. In education settings, self-regulated learning "is a core conceptual framework to understand the cognitive, motivational, and emotional aspects of learning" (Panadero, 2017). Our academic coaching model emphasizes self-understanding; improving students' self-regulation is another dimension of self-understanding. Based on how we've defined academic coaching thus far, note its natural fit in improving students' self-regulation as with this description by Zimmerman, "These learners are proactive in their efforts to learn because they are aware of their strengths and limitations and because they are guided by personally set goals and task-related strategies" (2002, pp. 65–66).

An academic coach, therefore, helps students understand the importance and techniques of becoming proactive in their approaches to learning and mastering skills. For example, an academic coach might ask a student to paint a picture of how they typically approach reading a chapter in their psychology textbook. One student response might be, "I read the assigned pages, and I underline and/or take notes when I think something is important." Full stop. This student does not seem to be deeply engaged in their reading process and is hoping that by getting to the end of the assignment, they will have then learned the material. An academic coach can prompt the student to think about how they might check their understanding of the text along the way, what steps they could take to remember key ideas well after they complete the reading, or how they could enhance their engagement when reading by perhaps setting a learning goal in advance or collecting questions as they proceed. In other words, through the collaborative relationship with their academic coach, a student can expand their skills as a self-regulated learner.

In addition to coaching students around regulating their learning process, academic coaches can help students improve their abilities to regulate how the changing state of emotions impact their academic experiences. No, academic coaches are not counselors or therapists, but they understand that students' affect, motivation, and self-concept can impact their academic success. Boekaerts and Cascallar (2006) detail how negative emotions and cognitions are triggered when a task is perceived as a threat. A student shares with their coach how their mood plummets before starting their weekly chemistry assignment because they just know it will be terribly hard. They feel frustrated by the length of time needed to work through the problems. They often get stuck, and they are certain that their peers don't experience the same level of challenges. This student will likely continue to struggle with their chemistry assignments due to the simultaneous presence of negative emotions and cognitions. An academic coach can work with the student to identify the feelings and thoughts that arise when faced with chemistry homework, and then brainstorm coping strategies to mitigate their impact. For example, the coach and student might collaboratively generate a written list of coping strategies for the student to refer to when they begin a homework session, such as using positive self-talk, reviewing PowerPoint slides from a lecture, or brewing their favorite cup of tea.

Over time, academic coaching can help students learn to practice monitoring their emotions and cognitions and adjust behaviors accordingly.

Self-regulation, whether focusing on study skills or on navigating the ups and downs of moods and emotions, is a critical factor in a student's overall success (Greene, 2018; Seli & Dembo, 2020). Academic coaching aims to strengthen students' ability to self-regulate, which leads them toward greater independence, flexibility, and agency in and out of the classroom.

The final piece of the academic coaching definition is that it empowers students to learn effective study skills. Academic coaching, after all, occurs in the context of educational settings. And students generally seek academic coaching because they want to improve some aspect of their academic performance. For example, they might be overwhelmed by and can't keep up with the volume of reading in their classes, or they don't know how to study for an upcoming geology midterm because their instructor does not provide a study guide, or they spent hours preparing for their world history exam but few of the exam questions seemed familiar and their grade was mediocre. Students may enter college without ever having needed to study before, or without understanding that the design of higher education is markedly different from what they'd been used to. The highly structured high school setting is replaced by a generally less structured college setting. Classes meet a few times per week instead of daily, instructors expect students to regularly engage and grapple with course content outside of the classroom, and final grades might be determined by just a few tests, papers, or projects. These are just a few of the enormous and potentially disorienting changes students face upon entering college. And these changes require new and additional study strategies. Thus, academic coaching seeks to guide students in figuring out what new tools they might need, and coaches provide support while students practice using them. We have relied on and have been influenced by many evidence-based models of effective learning and instructional strategies, and we highlight many of them in Chapters 9 and 10. To learn even more about these strategies, we encourage you to see the resources and references in those chapters.

WRAPPING UP

Academic coaching is a structured conversation that empowers students to become goal-centered and reflective while they develop improved academic and self-regulation skills. By understanding and embracing this definition, the rest of the academic coaching model will fall into place. The next set of chapters examines the guiding assumptions and beliefs a coach holds about students, the fundamental tools a coach uses to facilitate a conversation, and the four phases of a conversation. But a solid grasp of the definition of academic coaching is foundational.

REFERENCES

Boekaerts, M., & Cascallar, E. (2006). How far have we moved toward the integration of theory and practice in self-regulation? *Educational Psychology Review*, *18*(3), 199–210. https://doi.org/10.1007/s10648-006-9013-4

Greene, J. A. (2018). *Self-regulation in education*. Routledge.

Kimsey-House, H., Kimsey-House, K., Sandahl, P., & Whitworth, L. (2018). *Co-Active Coaching: The proven framework for transformative conversations at work and life* (4th ed.). Nicholas Brealey Publishing.

Locke, E. A. (1996). Motivation through conscious goal setting. *Applied and Preventive Psychology*, *5*(2), 117–124. https://doi.org/10.1016/S0962-1849(96)80005-9

Locke, E. A., & Latham, G. P. (1990). *A theory of goal setting & task performance*. Prentice-Hall, Inc.

Locke, E. A., & Latham, G. P. (2006). New directions in goal-setting theory. *Current Directions in Psychological Science*, *15*(5), 265–268. https://doi.org/10.1111/j.1467-8721.2006.00449.x

Nilson, L. B. (2013). *Creating self-regulated learners: Strategies to strengthen students' self-awareness and learning skills*. Stylus Publishing, LLC.

Panadero, E. (2017). A review of self-regulated learning: Six models and four directions for research. *Frontiers in Psychology*, *8*(422). https://doi.org/10.3389/fpsyg.2017.00422

Pintrich, P. (2000). The role of goal orientation in self-regulated learning. In M. Boekaerts, P. Pintrich, & M. Zeidner (Eds.), *Handbook of self-regulation* (pp. 451–502). Academic Press.

Schunk, D. H. (1989). Self-efficacy and cognitive skill learning. In C. Ames & R. Ames (Eds.), *Research on motivation in education: Goals and cognitions* (Vol. 3, pp. 13–44). Academic Press.

Seli, H., & Dembo, M. H. (2020). *Motivation and learning strategies for college success: A focus on self-regulated learning* (6th ed.). Routledge.

Zimmerman, B. J. (2002). Becoming a self-regulated learner: An overview. *Theory Into Practice*, *41*(2), 64–70. https://doi.org/10.1207/s15430421tip4102_2

Chapter 4

Fundamental Beliefs and Assumptions

Academic coaches approach every meeting with college students holding a specific set of beliefs and assumptions. These beliefs undergird academic coaching. The beliefs, which are inspired by the Co-Active® Coaching Model (Kimsey-House et al., 2018), provide a foundation for the skills and tools an academic coach uses to work with the full range of college students.[1] While they are simple to state, even an experienced academic coach works to consistently embody them in all student meetings.

Here are the five fundamental beliefs and assumptions we hold about students and academic coaching:

1. Students are "naturally creative, resourceful and whole" (Kimsey-House et al., 2018). They are not broken. They do not need to be fixed.
2. Students are the experts on their lives.
3. Focus on the student, not the problem.
4. Challenges are opportunities for growth.
5. Coaching is collaborative.

STUDENTS ARE "NATURALLY CREATIVE, RESOURCEFUL, AND WHOLE." THEY ARE NOT BROKEN. THEY DO NOT NEED TO BE FIXED

The first belief is paramount. It is the north star in our academic coaching sessions and has the biggest impact on our roles as coaches and how we interact with students. The heart of academic coaching centers on this belief, and without it, academic coaching may become a flat conversation or a consulting session. To examine it in greater detail, let's break it down into smaller chunks.

Naturally Creative

All people are incredibly creative. We might ascribe the creative label to artists, but every day each of us creates. Every time we speak, write, cook, interact with others, and play games we are creative. Navigating the contours of daily life mandates a reservoir of creative thoughts and actions.

What does this prodigious amount of creativity imply for academic coaching? For one, it means that coaches do not need to know the answers. Although students may want us to supply the answers for them, they proceed to devise their own unique ideas when told that we believe in their wisdom and given the time and space to think creatively. Students regularly generate novel approaches to common issues like time management that we would not have imagined on our own. One student may carry around an index card in their shirt pocket that spells out their daily schedule and to-dos, while another employs a system of calendar alerts to indicate when they need to start their biology reading and another writes with erasable markers on the bathroom mirror. When their creativity is unleashed, college students can come up with an amazing array of approaches to studying and learning (McGuire & McGuire, 2015).

If we as academic coaches do not take advantage of students' own innate ingenuity, we are squandering a vast resource and creating a relationship where students may over-rely on us rather than develop faith in their own abilities.

Resourceful and Whole

Perhaps every generation has grumbled about the lack of resilience of the proverbial "kids these days." But today's students are inherently resourceful. They have navigated many challenges before an academic coaching conversation and have the capability to find ways to overcome challenges and difficulties. At one point our students began high school and had to learn their way around a new building, class schedule, and peers. They've learned how to develop and sustain friendships and juggle the challenges of high school while handling the arduous task of applying to college. Tapping into their own, inner resources is not new to students as they've done so their entire lives. While a student might feel overwhelmed by unfamiliar college challenges—improving study strategies, managing daily life without adult supervision, writing research papers (Conley, 2007; Quinn & Maitland, 2011)—an academic coach reminds them of their innate resourcefulness, resilience, and slate of past accomplishments. Students are then encouraged to believe in the possibility of new growth and learning.

Resourcefulness, resilience, and grit can be developed (Duckworth, 2016; Dweck, 2006). Although some students may have more direct access to their own resourcefulness or possess greater confidence in their abilities to navigate difficult times, we maintain that everyone is naturally resourceful. By holding that belief about students, we help them grow confidence in their own capabilities to overcome challenges.

The dictionary defines whole as something that is "unbroken or undamaged." Therefore, in academic coaching, we focus on strengths, possibility, and growth.

Whole means that students are capable and competent. Whole means students can start changing today. Students can move forward. Although students are whole, they might not always feel that way. At times, we all feel weak, defeated, and perhaps even broken. As academic coaches, we maintain the belief of wholeness on behalf of the student even when they feel lost or hopeless. Having someone who believes you are inherently whole creates an atmosphere where growth is possible and is one of the great gifts of academic coaching. Eric Garcia, who writes about academic coaching at UNC-Chapel Hill in his book about autism, gave his book the title *We're Not Broken* (2021).

Students Are Not Broken. They Do Not Need to Be Fixed

The final two sentences of the first belief speak to the sometimes-radical nature of academic coaching as a form of student support in higher education. These sentences demand that the coach takes a stand for the student's creativity, resourcefulness, and wholeness in spite of the current difficulties they may be encountering.

Some higher education professionals believe, whether consciously or unconsciously, that students really do need to be fixed. Students sometimes see themselves this way, too. A dynamic can be created in which staff and faculty, with a wealth of knowledge and experience, assume the role of guiding, directing, and even telling students what to do because of their perceptions that students need fixing.

When we as professionals believe that students are indeed broken and need to be fixed, we choose to focus on what is wrong with the student and become something like an academic car mechanic. We kick the tires, run some tests, make repairs, and then send the student car back out on the road. We do the diagnostic work rather than help the student learn how to independently analyze and improve their own situation. So, what happens if the student's car breaks down the next day or gets stuck in a rut? Does the academic car mechanic approach promote resilience, empowerment, independence, and growth? No! When the coach analyzes problems and makes decisions for the student then the responsibility for the outcome of those decisions, good or bad, remains with the coach. The academic car mechanic approach also suppresses rather than promotes the development of a student's metacognitive and self-regulatory learning abilities.

Academic coaches work to keep the agency with students as much as possible, which means we must believe in their innate wholeness, resourcefulness, and creativity. Yes, they stumble and meet challenges and sometimes even fail. But this doesn't make them broken and in need of our fixing. This makes them human.

STUDENTS ARE THE EXPERTS ON THEIR LIVES

The second fundamental belief closely relates to the first. Let's take the complement of this belief: academic coaches are not the experts on students' lives. What does that mean? We all have expertise. That expertise might include reading, writing, learning differences, transportation planning, or biology. However, all students know much more about themselves and their life circumstances than we do. Students come into our spaces with rich histories.

Some may interpret these beliefs as meaning that students have everything they need inside, and we just need to pull it out of them. That is not true. At times, all students can benefit from hearing about new evidence-based study strategies or other campus resources. And, yes, students can even benefit from an occasional direct suggestion (not a mandate). However, academic coaches hold the firm belief that because students know themselves best, their self-knowledge must be part of the equation in all aspects of analyzing their situation, goal-setting, planning, and defining their next steps. Just how an academic coach can contribute their specific knowledge and experience to a coaching conversation without being directive is something we cover in detail in later chapters.

The belief that students are the experts on their lives reshapes the relationship between academic professional and student from hierarchical to collaborative. A coach saying, "I honestly do not know what will work best for you, so let's work together to figure out some approaches," is a wonderfully common component of academic coaching.

In academic coaching, we believe in and promote student agency. Aligning with the theoretical frameworks of self-authorship (Baxter Magolda, 2001) and self-determination (Deci & Ryan, 1985; Field & Hoffman, 1994), we maintain that students are the authors of their lives. And as academic coaches, we are particularly focused on promoting the self-authoring of each student's life.

While students are the experts on their lives, this does not mean a coach is a passive participant without expertise. We all bring extensive experience and expertise to an academic coaching conversation. We participate actively in helping students identify their goals, better understand their strengths and growth areas, and expand and refine their learning strategies. All these efforts occur within the framework of a student being the expert on their own life.

FOCUS ON THE STUDENT, NOT THE PROBLEM

For all of the talk about student-centeredness (O'Neill & McMullin, 2005; Revuluri, 2021; Taylor, 2013; Wright, 2011), higher education remains largely focused on problems and accomplishments. Failing chemistry. Winning a prestigious award. Graduating in four years. Students are part of those descriptions, but they exist tangentially.

In academic coaching the student is at the center. This may sound both cliché and elicit a "duh," but it is critical and more difficult to implement in day-to-day work than it may seem. Say a student comes into our offices because it is their first semester at college, and they have gotten all Ds and Fs on exams. For even an experienced academic coach, it can be easy to focus on the problem and not the person. We can say, "let's improve these test scores" and if we are not careful the grades become central, and the person fades into the background. As academic coaches, we broaden our lens and take the time to build rapport and learn about the person sitting with us. This wide focus allows us to see the bigger picture of who this student is and how they are managing college overall.

Academic coaching is challenging. Certainly, if a student wants to work on improving test scores that can be the organizing topic of conversation, but we must remember the person. And why does that matter? If we neglect the person, the academic coaching conversation might miss critical components to the student's circumstances, such as lack of sleep, missing friends from home, classes that are uninteresting, or food insecurity. Or maybe by focusing on the whole person and not the problem we discover that the student really wants to work on something else entirely. The desire to "improve test scores" might just be the entry point into our office and the conversation.

In academic coaching we are working on multiple temporal fronts. We can work with a student on study strategies to get a better Chemistry exam grade. But the student's long-term academic growth is also front and center. These skills, strategies, approaches, and learnings can benefit a student now and in the future. Ultimately, we aim to grow the agency and ability of students so that they can coach themselves and improve their abilities to self-regulate their learning. These aims support broader higher education goals of developing empowered learners (House & Frymier, 2009). If we focus only on the problem at the expense of the student then we stray back into the role of academic car mechanics, meaning that students must rely on us both now and in the future. Let's not just talk about student-centeredness, let's embody the belief that students, and not anything less, are the focus of our work.

CHALLENGES ARE OPPORTUNITIES FOR GROWTH

In the midst of an immense personal struggle, someone pointing out that our current challenge is actually an opportunity for growth can make us throw up our hands in exasperation. What could be "good" about a low test grade or being on probation? While the sentiment that challenges are opportunities for growth may feel impossible in the moment and may sound trite out of context, it is undeniably true. When do we grow? When do we make possibility a reality? We can guarantee that growth almost never happens during those days that resemble a luxurious visit to the beach with placid seas and a lemon-yellow sun. Those are the days to bask in accomplishment, where everything goes smoothly and easily while we take a nap.

Sports tryouts. Living in a new place. A dissertation. A business failure. Fs on Math exams. None of these endeavors are particularly fun. But these are the times for growth. As academic coaches we may ask, "Unbelievable as it may seem at the moment, can you imagine a possible gift here?" We define failure not as getting a low grade but as failing to take the opportunity to learn from the situation. We view success in both learning and perseverance. If we gave up every time, we weren't able to get something right, we wouldn't be able to do anything. We certainly wouldn't be able to walk or eat or speak. Let alone take derivatives or balance equations. Carol Dweck's work on a growth versus a fixed mindset (2006) parallels this academic coaching belief that when challenges are viewed as life's best learning opportunities, we can stop approaching them with dread. Every student will continue to encounter challenges, but when coaches help students believe in the transformative growth that can result from challenges, they are on their way to becoming competent adults capable of weathering life's storms.

If everything is easy, chances are you aren't learning much.

COACHING IS COLLABORATIVE

All the preceding beliefs culminate in the fact that collaboration is the heart of academic coaching. Collaboration means that both the academic coach and the student have responsibility and play active roles. To use another transportation metaphor, in academic coaching we try to keep the student in the driver's seat as much as possible. The coach is in the passenger seat, ready to help navigate if needed, but always encourages the student to take the wheel. The student retains the agency for the ultimate decision of where to go, how to get there, and the underlying reason for the journey in the first place. Collaboration directly supports student agency and learner empowerment (Wells & Jones, 2018).

The academic coach in the passenger seat is an active collaborator. The coach does not say, "I'm going to take a nap. Wake me up when you finish your honors thesis." Instead, the academic coach helps the student refine their goals, stay on track, reflect on the various routes available, honestly evaluate progress, and even offer a suggestion. As tempting as it might be, the academic coach resists taking the wheel and making decisions about how to proceed with the thesis. In the spirit of collaboration an academic coach may say, "Some students have found it helpful to meet up with others working on honors theses and just write. Would that be something you'd like to try?" Fully embodying all the previous beliefs, an academic coach has no attachment to these suggestions and is ready to get in the passenger seat at the next session no matter whether the plan was implemented, successful or not. If the student does not seem to be progressing between sessions, the coach asks permission to point this out so that together they can explore what may be behind a period of idleness. Believing in and trusting the academic coaching process, a coach helps students continually design and evaluate the path that leads to accomplishing their goals and dreams while learning about themselves along the way.

There are many elements that affect whether an academic coaching conversation feels more or less collaborative. One aspect to consider is the spatial arrangement of your office or meeting space since it contributes to an environment that can be more (or less) welcoming and inclusive to college students (Hogan & Sathy, 2022, p. 167). If possible, we suggest working at small tables with college students with the computer safely away from the meeting area. This arrangement contrasts with a more-traditional office space where a large desk separates the student from the professional where the professional can see their computer, which is obscured from the student. We want academic coaching to be more collaborative and less hierarchical, so take some time to assess how your space can be configured to accentuate the collaborative nature of academic coaching.

WRAPPING UP

These five beliefs provide the foundation for our work as academic coaches. Without them, an academic coaching session can be just another friendly conversation, an instructional session, or perhaps even a relationship that inadvertently inhibits a student from growing and developing agency. In all circumstances, even with the most difficult students, we have seen these beliefs become the catalyst that has facilitated them to slowly take charge of their lives and conquer the new world of college. As coaches who hold these beliefs daily, we have witnessed hundreds of students directly face their challenges and experience transformative growth.

When an academic coach faces a difficult appointment or finds that a coaching session isn't going as well as they'd like, we suggest channeling these beliefs. Academic coaching becomes easier and more effective when you embody the beliefs that the student is "naturally creative, resourceful, and whole" (Kimsey-House et al., 2018), the expert on their life, has a whole lifetime of experiences to build from, and can be transformed from their current challenges. The academic coaching relationship is a true collaboration where both parties take active roles in service of facilitating student development.

Emerging from these fundamental beliefs are a set of academic coaching tools and skills. These fundamental tools comprise what a professional is actually doing during academic coaching. And they are the subject of the next chapter.

NOTE

1 It's worth noting that while we were both trained and certified through the Co-Active®
Training Institute (CTI), many of the beliefs and variations of the beliefs discussed in
this chapter appear throughout coaching. The International Coaching Federation (ICF),
for example, as part of its core competencies says that coaches must embody a "coaching mindset" that is "open, curious, flexible and client-centered" (International Coaching
Federation, n.d.).

REFERENCES

Baxter Magolda, M. B. (2001). *Making their own way: Narratives for transforming higher
education to promote self-development*. Stylus Publishing.

Conley, D. (2007). *Toward a more comprehensive conception of college readiness*. Educational
Policy Improvement Center.

Deci, E. L., & Ryan, R. M. (1985). *Intrinsic motivation and self-determination in human
behavior*. Plenum Press.

Duckworth, A. (2016). *Grit: The power of passion and perseverance*. Scribner.

Dweck, C. S. (2006). *Mindset: The new psychology of success*. Ballantine Books.

Field, S., & Hoffman, A. (1994). Development of a model for self-determination. *Career
Development for Exceptional Individuals*, *17*(2), 159–169.

Garcia, E. (2021). *We're not broken: Changing the autism conversation*. Harvest.

Hogan, K. A., & Sathy, V. (2022). *Inclusive teaching: Strategies for promoting equity in the
college classroom*. West Virginia University Press.

House, M. L., & Frymier, A. B. (2009). The role of student characteristics and teacher
behaviors in students' learner empowerment. *Communication Education*, *58*(1),
35–53. https://doi.org/10.1080/03634520802237383

International Coaching Federation. (n.d.). *ICF core competencies*. Retrieved July 10,
2022, from https://coachingfederation.org/credentials-and-standards/core-
competencies

Kimsey-House, H., Kimsey-House, K., Sandahl, P., & Whitworth, L. (2018). *Co-Active
Coaching: The proven framework for transformative conversations at work and life* (4th ed.).
Nicholas Brealey Publishing.

McGuire, S. Y., & McGuire, S. (2015). *Teach students how to learn: Strategies you can
incorporate into any course to improve student metacognition, study skills, and motivation*.
Stylus Publishing.

O'Neill, G., & McMullin, B. (2005). Student-centered learning: What does it mean for
students and lecturers? In G. O'Neill, S. Moore, & B. McMullin (Eds.), *Emerging
issues in the practice of university learning and teaching* (pp. 27–36). AISHE.

Quinn, P. O., & Maitland, T. L. (2011). *On your own: A college readiness guide for teens with
ADHD/LD*. Magination Press.

Revuluri, S. (2021). Student-centered learning and teaching–Lessons from academic support. In S. Hoidn & M. Klemencic (Eds.), *The Routledge International handbook of student-centered learning and teaching in higher education* (pp. 414–423). Routledge.

Taylor, J. (2013). What is student centredness and is it enough? *International Journal of the First Year in Higher Education, 4*(2), 39–48. https://doi.org/10.5204/intjfyhe.v4i1.168

Wells, H., & Jones, A. (2018). Learning to change: The rationale for the use of motivational interviewing in higher education. *Innovations in Education and Teaching International, 55*(1), 111–118. https://doi.org/10.1080/14703297.2016.1198714

Wright, G. B. (2011). Student-centered learning in higher education. *International Journal of Teaching and Learning in Higher Education, 23*(3), 92–97.

Chapter 5

Fundamental Tools

In building this model of academic coaching, we began with a foundation of the definition, scaffolded it with the fundamental beliefs and assumptions, and in this chapter, we move forward with what an academic coach does when working with college students. These are the fundamental tools, which are adapted from the Co-Active® Coaching Model (Kimsey-House et al., 2018). We know that academic coaches will do many different things and employ a wide variety of skills and approaches in their work with college students, but these are the foundational four that undergird the practice.

- Ask open-ended questions
- Be curious
- Listen fully
- Manage self

ASK OPEN-ENDED QUESTIONS

The paramount belief in academic coaching is that "students are naturally creative, resourceful and whole" (Kimsey-House et al., 2018), they are not broken and don't need to be fixed. Likewise, there is a paramount tool that rises above all others in terms of importance. The keystone method of facilitating academic coaching is asking open-ended questions. All other elements of academic coaching radiate out from this main hub.

What makes asking open-ended questions so critical to academic coaching? Academic coaching is a conversation between a coach and student centered on the student learning, growing, and achieving their academic goals. Academic coaching upends or at least helps flatten traditional hierarchical roles and power dynamics and brings the student into a greater position of power and agency. In higher education, we often talk about being student-centered, strengths-based, and meeting students where they are. Asking open-ended questions helps accomplish all those things. Open-ended

DOI: 10.4324/9781003291879-7

questions are powerful. And, indeed, they are often referred to as powerful questions (Kimsey-House et al., 2018; Stoltzfus, 2008; van Nieuwerburgh, 2020; Whitmore, 2017).

One of the primary benefits of asking open-ended questions is that it keeps the focus of the conversation on the student. A coach asking open-ended questions, by definition, is not giving advice, sharing stories, telling someone what to do, or talking about their own life. Open-ended questions move the emphasis of the conversation to the student. When an academic coach asks a student, "What's important to you?" "What works best for you?" "What do you want to do?" the conversational ground shifts in the direction of the student. When these questions are truly open-ended and not leading or judgmental or looking for a specific answer, they communicate a number of messages to the student:

- I see you.
- I hear you.
- I care about what you say.
- I believe you.
- I believe in you.

Having someone believe these things about you is an incredibly powerful experience.

Asking open-ended questions promotes self-reflection and learning. One of the fundamental beliefs is that we are coaching the student and not the problem. Academic coaching functions on multiple temporal levels. Sure, most students come to us because of a nearer-term goal or challenge. We want to help students prepare for their next exam or improve their time management over the coming weeks. We also aim for long-term academic development, and a primary way to promote growth is through self-reflection and learning powered by asking open-ended questions.

Questions are often asked to obtain information. These are the classic who, what, where, when, and why that are often referred to as reporter questions. While open-ended questions elicit information, more importantly, they get students to pause, think, and reflect. Our students are busy and might not have the time or opportunity to think about their learning. We ask students what might seem like basic questions, "How do you study?" or "How do you approach reading?" or "What's the purpose of taking notes?" Many students might not have considered these questions before. For many of us, our approaches to learning go unexamined without assessing their effectiveness or how we might modify them to support our learning.

Asking open-ended questions also helps make academic coaching a collaborative conversation. We interchange the terms academic coaching appointments and academic coaching conversations for a reason. We want these meetings to be conversations. And not just conversations, we want these to be collaborative conversations with two active participants. When talking with students or in other areas of life, notice what shuts a conversation down and what opens it up. Closed-ended questions generally result in one-word answers, and it's challenging to maintain a conversation for any length of time if a person is saying one or two words at a time.

What makes open-ended questions open-ended? While it might seem obvious, these questions contain specific elements:

- There are many potential answers.
- The coach is open to hearing a wide variety of answers.
- The question is asked without judgment.
- The question is asked from a place of curiosity.

In working to apply the academic coaching model, many university faculty and staff grapple with making the transition from providing advice and telling students what to do to asking open-ended questions. One of the challenges that some people encounter is being okay with and prepared for a wide variety of student answers. Asking open-ended questions is not a ploy to lead students to a certain answer a coach wants to hear. Students are smart. If we think there is a "right" answer, they will often try to provide us with that right answer, even if it's within the context of an ostensibly open-ended question.

While it is technically possible to ask a question that is both open-ended and judgmental, such as "Why did you do that?", within the context of academic coaching it's important for questions to be asked in a non-judgmental manner. Leaning on the fundamental beliefs can help in asking open-ended questions without judgments. Another strategy that is helpful in asking open-ended questions is to begin with the word "What" such as "What do you make of that?"

Open-ended questions that begin with the word "What," as you'll see in the list below, typically help shift the focus of the conversation to the student, promote self-reflection and learning, and are non-judgmental. Conversely, questions that begin with "Why" can often sound judgmental even when we intend them otherwise. Of course, tone and delivery matter a lot.

Here are some favorite open-ended academic coaching questions:

- What's next?
- What's the gift in this situation?
- What have you learned from X?
- How can you apply this to future situations?
- What's your assessment of X?
- What would help you reach this goal?
- What does this say about you as a student?
- I know what X means to me; what does it mean to you?

- What would an ideal picture of the situation look like?
- What would your future self say about the situation?
- If you could boil this down, what is the most important part?
- What might you think about this one year from now? Five years?
- What would you tell your best friend if they were facing the same situation?

Here are some great open-ended questions that aren't technically questions.

- Tell me more.
- That's really interesting, and I would love to hear you expand.
- I'm happy to share my ideas, but I'd like to hear your thoughts first.
- Walk me through…

LISTEN FULLY

One of the great gifts of academic coaching is that a student is present with a person dedicated to their learning, growth, and success. Rarely, do we encounter others who are fully in the present with their complete attention on us and in support of us? As the Co-Active® Coaching book states, "To be truly listened to is a striking experience, partly because it is so rare" (Kimsey-House et al., 2018, p. 37).

As the words imply, listening fully moves beyond simply listening and even beyond active listening to a holistic approach centered on the present and the person (Kimsey-House et al., 2018; Whitmore, 2017). We listen to the words said, words not said, body language, and other information emanating from the student.

Listening fully, of course, involves a lot of active listening to what students are saying. One of the main elements of active listening is paraphrasing (van Nieuwerburgh, 2020). We hear what the student says and then put it in our own words. We also use the skill of articulation (covered in Chapter 7) to verbalize what we are hearing or seeing.

Speaking of seeing, Listening fully includes using visual information that we see when working with students. A student might come into our office and never put their bag on the floor, clutching it tightly. Or a student might say something while having a facial expression that doesn't quite match up. In this case, we could say, "I noticed that when you said you failed an exam it looked like you were smiling. Can you talk more about that?" A student might come into our offices seeming especially confident or relaxed. We don't want to assume anything or make prejudgments, but all this information is helpful in generating open-ended questions and working collaboratively with students.

Listening fully is directly connected with asking open-ended questions. Academic coaching is a conversation that is iterative and recursive, it keeps building upon itself with the information emerging, continually updating both a student and coach's understanding and experience. As elaborated upon in the preceding section, if a question is truly open-ended, then a coach is open to a vast spectrum of possible responses. Since there are, by design, an almost unlimited range of answers in response to an open-ended question, a coach listening fully to what a student says is critical to continue moving the conversation forward. This does not mean a coach has to be perfect, but they do need to be present. A coach can always paraphrase, reflect, and check in. We can say, "Okay, here's what I'm hearing you saying. Does that sound about right?"

Student Language

One approach to enhance your professional listening is to pay more attention to and incorporate student language into your coaching. A student in an academic coaching appointment might say that they were like a flower needing sunlight and water. A coach could then ask, "In the midst of studying for midterms, what does the flower need to stay healthy?" In this way, the academic coach signals that they are paying close attention to what the student is saying and then furthers the metaphor by incorporating that language into the fabric of a conversation.

The mirroring of language, words, and phrasing can be even more simple and direct than picking up on a student's figurative language. A student may describe the past week of college as chaotic. A coach can then mirror back the language. "What would be helpful in making things less chaotic?" Even if a student doesn't consciously realize that we are using their language, it's an implicit signal that we are listening fully and engaged with what they say.

A student's language, words, and phrasing can also be a useful route of exploration, clarification, and reflection in the process of asking open-ended questions. One foundational aspect of academic coaching is checking our assumptions. A student can say something like, "My main problem is procrastination" or "I'm way behind on my paper." While it's easy and understandable to assume we know what the student is referring to, these situations are opportunities to ask open-ended, reflective questions. We can say, "I know what procrastination means for me, but what does that look like for you?" or, even more straightforward, "What does 'way behind' mean to you?" While these questions help a coach gather more information and get them on the same page as the student, there are times when the questions help the student clarify and gain a better understanding of what they mean.

Whiteboards

Many academic coaches are frequent users of whiteboards. We recommend using whiteboards rather than taking personal notes during an appointment. Why? As underscored in the academic coaching definition as well as the fundamental beliefs, academic coaching is a collaborative practice. Taking personal, private notes during an appointment can undermine that collaborative nature, potentially making it feel to the student as if we are evaluating them. In contrast, writing on a whiteboard makes the notes communal. Academic coaches use whiteboards to capture a student's language or ideas. We also invite students to write. We suggest, "How about you write that down?" We aim to have the space be as collaborative as possible.

A former student of Marc's published a memoir about his college experience, including the whiteboard's value to academic coaching sessions:

> Sometimes I would utter a word or phrase, and it would catch Marc's attention. He would then grab a marker and write my words on the whiteboard. By the end of my rambling, he would point to these keyboards and phrases that I had uttered. He was showing me I had the answer within myself.
>
> When I realized that, the meetings involved less of Marc writing on the whiteboard, and instead I grabbed the markers and scribbled on the whiteboard as we navigated through my thoughts and analyzed ways to accomplish tasks. I wrote in all twelve colors of marker that Marc's office had to offer.
>
> (Bolding, 2021, p. 23)

BE CURIOUS

For many of us, we work in higher education in roles as staff or faculty because of our interest in people. Education is inherently interpersonal. Coaching provides an opportunity and indeed necessitates cultivating curiosity (Kimsey-House et al., 2018; van Nieuwerburgh, 2020). Each appointment, each conversation is tailored to the individual at a specific time. As higher education professionals we meet with and work with numerous students. With time and experience and often overloaded schedules and workloads resulting from decreasing funding and increasing responsibilities, it can be easy and understandable to start categorizing students into standard archetypes. "I've seen this before," we say to ourselves before launching into well-rehearsed advice and wisdom. We get it. We've been there. Without consistent attention (see the upcoming section "Manage Self"), we can slip into robo-coaching and professional autopilot.

Let's take a minute to assess the potential impacts on students if we go into robo-coaching or professional autopilot. When we meet with a student where we assume we know the context, background, and path forward, we lose track of the individual. Students are smart and can discern when another person isn't interested in what they have to say. The experience can be disempowering. A student may apologize for bothering us, even though working with them is our professional responsibility. In such situations, students can become nameless faces or faceless names. And these impersonal experiences may discourage students from seeking out other campus resources.

Contrast professional autopilot with a student-centered approach suffused with being curious. In such an interaction we are there with the student, delving into what makes that student unique in terms of their hopes, dreams, background, and contexts. One of the themes of this book is that academic coaching and a coach approach offer a tangible method of student-centered work in higher education. Being curious helps make our work even more student-centered.

There tend to be some general patterns for students coming to academic coaching. Many students encounter challenges, for example, with transitioning from high school to college. But even within similar situations, there remains a unique individual with their own past, present, and future. Hopes and dreams. Strengths, difficulties, interests, backgrounds, and contexts. In academic coaching, we want to avoid making assumptions.

Our friend and colleague Dr. Theresa Maitland, who helped bring coaching to UNC-Chapel Hill and was integral to the development of this academic coaching model used to say, "Curiosity is the rich, organic soil from which open-ended questions grow." Let's cultivate that curiosity!

MANAGE SELF

Sometimes during an academic coaching session, it may appear that the coach might not be doing much. They ask questions, listen fully, and engage with the student in a collaborative conversation, but if academic coaching is proceeding along as designed, the student is doing more of the talking and work. And by work that means the student is taking the lead in reflecting on the topic at hand, coming up with potential options for moving forward, and ultimately creating an action plan of next steps. A coach managing themselves is critical to a successful coaching conversation (Kimsey-House et al., 2018).

Even if a coach is primarily sitting there listening and asking questions, following the academic coaching model is hard work. We often refer to manage self as an "under the hood" tool because it can be difficult to see. Manage self is frequently the tool that presents the most difficulty for many coaches and needs to be attended to regularly even with years or decades of experience.

Refraining (aka Academic Coaching Is Not "Here Is What You Need to Do")

Manage self is such an important and difficult tool in large part because academic coaching represents a fundamental shift in the way many higher education professionals work with students. Many people new to academic coaching report they find it hard to resist telling the student what to do, providing advice, and offering personal stories or examples. Within this context, one of the core things an academic coach does is refrain. This doesn't mean we withhold helpful information, strategies, or resources, which we'll cover in greater detail later. But it does mean we put the student first and our own agendas well in the back.

Refraining from telling students what to do is one of the most important aspects of academic coaching. The phrase "telling students what to do" may sound a bit harsh. A gentler version of this is providing advice to students. But are they that different? Think of a typical meeting between a university staff or faculty member and student. In most cases, there's a significant power imbalance. The higher education professional is typically older with more credentials and occupying a position of authority. Students are used to being told what to do by adults within their educational contexts. So, at the end of the day, there's likely minimal difference between "Here's what I think you should do…" or "Here's what I would do…." and "Here's what you need to do…." We often describe a coaching conversation as friendly but not a conversation between friends. When talking with friends, providing advice and relating personal stories are standard features, but in academic coaching we strive to refrain from giving advice.

Another element of refraining is allowing a conversation to evolve just slightly more slowly, allowing students to fill gaps, make connections and learn from the moment. One common occurrence during an academic coaching appointment is for a student to make a statement that we agree with and support. For example, while discussing preparations for an upcoming exam they might say, "I should start studying earlier." At this moment, it's understandable to be enthusiastic and say something like, "That's great! When should you start studying?" But before jumping to the next step, it's helpful to pause and explore the situation a little more. You could ask, "How would starting earlier help your exam prep?" While the answer to such a question may seem obvious, it's useful for students to unpack their statements and assertions to enhance learning and deepen understanding. A student may say they should start studying earlier because that's what they think that they should do or that's what they've been told to do. Even the simple question, "How would starting earlier help?" could unlock thoughtful discussions of spacing out studying, study strategies, using resources, and more.

Being Present

Manage self is multi-faceted. Being present and returning to the present moment is another main category for this academic coaching tool. We lead busy, complicated lives. On any given day, we might have imminent deadlines, personal issues to attend to, and competing priorities. In academic coaching, it's critical to set those things aside for the moment and be in the present with the student. Our interpersonal work is undermined if we are distracted and distant. Inevitably, some different thoughts will sneak in. We'll remember that we need to eat lunch or return a phone call or make arrangements for picking up a child from school. That's okay. But when these kinds of thoughts arrive it's time to set them aside and return to the student in front of us.

Practically, we can help set ourselves up for success in staying and returning to the present when working with students by making sure we are taking care of ourselves. Sometimes we refer to this as managing our physical, mental, and emotional selves. Are we making sure to eat during the day and drink water? Do we take breaks? Do we allow ourselves transition times? Do we try to set aside our professional obligations when outside of work to allow ourselves time to relax and recharge? As higher education professionals, often working in contexts with ever-increasing workloads, the ability to take care of ourselves may seem like a distant dream. However, pause for a second and think about the suggestion you might give a student in a similar situation with nary a moment to spare. You'd likely encourage them to make sure they are prioritizing their own well-being. We believe we are all deserving of such self-compassion and care.

Biases and Lenses

Every academic coach has their own unique personal context and history. We each have our own identities as well as social identities ascribed to us. As academic coaches, it is critical to become familiar with our own biases and perspectives. We must know our own lenses and how we view the world and be cognizant of their potential impacts on our work with students. Examining one's own biases is an important part of supporting diversity, equity, and inclusion efforts in higher education (Addy et al., 2021; Carnes et al., 2012; Cuyjet et al., 2016; Puckett & Lind, 2020) as well as coaching (Aguilar, 2020; Baron & Azizollah, 2018). Being honest and open with ourselves is essential. For many of us, it might feel uncomfortable to acknowledge and examine our own personal biases and lenses. However, by knowing more about ourselves, we will be better able to manage self during academic coaching conversations.

One core element of academic coaching is resisting assumptions. Assumptions in their more harmful forms can become prejudices and stereotypes. While academic coaching is highly customized and individualized, it occurs within larger societal frameworks including structural inequality and systemic racism and discrimination. As academic coaches, we consistently employ the fundamental tool of manage self in resisting assumptions. College students are incredibly diverse. We can be much more effective coaches by making fewer assumptions about the students with whom we work and instead ask more curiosity-driven, open-ended questions. We discuss academic coaching with the great diversity of college students in more detail in Chapter 12.

WRAPPING UP

Academic coaches utilize a wide variety of tools and approaches, but the four skills described in this chapter will be part of every coaching conversation. While coaching can seem complicated, and it can be easy to start overthinking what your next move should be, returning to these fundamentals will almost always serve you well. If you are asking open-ended questions, listening fully, being curious, and managing self while embodying the fundamental beliefs then you will likely be doing an excellent job of coaching. We'll add more tools in Chapter 7 by covering expanded coaching skills.

The next chapter details the four phases of an academic coaching conversation. There's a general pace and contour of an academic coaching conversation, which will adjust based on how much time we have to work with a student and other contextual factors. Our responsibility in academic coaching is to make sure the conversation is matching up and proceeding within the overarching academic coaching framework. One important element of the definition of academic coaching is that it's a structured conversation, so let's move into examining that structure and the four phases of an academic coaching conversation.

REFERENCES

Addy, T. M., Dube, D., Mitchell, K. A., & SoRelle, M. E. (2021). *What inclusive instructors do: Principles and practices for excellence in college teaching.* Stylus Publishing.

Aguilar, E. (2020). *Coaching for equity: Conversations that change practice.* Jossey-Bass.

Baron, H., & Azizollah, H. (2018). Coaching and diversity. In S. Palmer & A. Whybrow (Eds.), *Handbook of coaching psychology: A guide for practitioners* (2nd ed., pp. 500–511). Routledge.

Bolding, J. D. (2021). *We're all gonna die one day.* Barnes & Noble Press.

Carnes, M., Devine, P. G., Isaac, C., Manwell, L. B., Ford, C. E., Byars-Winston, A., Fine, E., & Sheridan, J. (2012). Promoting institutional change through bias literacy. *Journal of Diversity in Higher Education, 5*(2), 63. https://doi.org/10.1037/a0028128

Cuyjet, M. J., Linder, C., Howard-Hamilton, M. F., & Cooper, D. L. (Eds.). (2016). *Multiculturalism on campus: Theory, models, and practices for understanding diversity and creating inclusion* (2nd ed.). Stylus Publishing.

Kimsey-House, H., Kimsey-House, K., Sandahl, P., & Whitworth, L. (2018). *Co-Active Coaching: The proven framework for transformative conversations at work and life* (4th ed.). Nicholas Brealey Publishing.

Puckett, T., & Lind, N. S. (Eds.). (2020). *Cultural competence in higher education*. Emerald Publishing Limited.

Stoltzfus, T. (2008). *Coaching questions: A coach's guide to powerful asking skills*. Coach22 Bookstore LLC.

van Nieuwerburgh, C. (2020). *An introduction to coaching skills: A practical guide* (3rd ed.). SAGE Publications Ltd.

Whitmore, J. (2017). *Coaching for performance: The principles and practice of coaching and leadership* (5th ed.). Nicholas Brealey Publishing.

Chapter 6

Phases of an Academic Coaching Conversation

We are ready for the next piece of the academic coaching model. With an under-standing of the fundamental coaching beliefs and assumptions and armed with the fundamental coaching tools used by a coach, the next step is to learn how to facilitate a coaching conversation.

A coaching conversation follows a concrete structure. The structure is criti-cal because it provides a clear framework in which to utilize the coaching tools as well as move the student to action. Effective academic coaches need to under-stand the fundamental coaching beliefs and must use fundamental coaching tools, such as asking open-ended questions. However, these beliefs and tools need to be applied systematically while coaching. Without a technique to facilitate a coach-ing session, a conversation can be aimless. Imagine you've packed your car for a vacation; it's bursting with luggage, tote bags, bicycles, and a cooler. You grab the keys and start the ignition and then it dawns on you: where exactly are we going? You've gathered the components for a vacation, but without a destination, the components amount to a just bunch of stuff in your car.

Coaching conversations need a destination. Asking open-ended questions and structure provide the necessary path to reach the destination.

An academic coaching conversation is divided into four distinct phases: set the agenda, self-reflect and learn, explore options and actions, and design and commit to plans. For the most part, these phases follow a sequential order, but as you will see, coaches can and do often toggle between phases.

PHASE ONE: SET THE AGENDA

At the start of every academic coaching session, the coach and student deter-mine the focus of the conversation. This focus, or agenda, lays the foundation for the entire session and steers the coach and the student into a clear direction. A clear direction is essential; without it, a coaching conversation can poten-tially drift aimlessly. Aimless conversations aren't inherently bad—who hasn't enjoyed meandering discussions with friends and family? But while discussions in coaching can take unexpected turns, the coach works to ensure that these turns are in service of addressing the student's agenda.

Setting the agenda can seem deceptively easy, as if it's a matter of just asking students what they'd like to focus on and then expecting them to articulate concisely. Sure, sometimes students very clearly want coaching on a defined topic, such as the best way to use flashcards for a foreign language class. There's not necessarily a lot of room for interpretation regarding a coaching topic there. But agenda-setting can sometimes be tricky because students often grapple with overlapping issues, they bring up an overly broad idea, or they are simply overwhelmed and don't know how to begin.

An academic coach must spend a few minutes listening fully to the student and asking clarifying questions to arrive at a coachable issue in the allotted time frame. And by coachable, we mean a topic that is narrow enough to know where to dig in, but open enough so that there's room to explore.

Let's look at an example.

A student says their coaching agenda is to create a system to keep up with the pace and rigor of reading for their American Literature class because they are on the verge of falling significantly behind. This topic might seem straightforward enough, but through curiosity and collaboration, the student and coach must first understand what is driving the issue. Is there something about the nature of this kind of reading that is particularly hard for the student? Maybe this is the first time they are required to analyze literature beyond the surface level. Is there something about how the student approaches reading for this class? In other words, are they utilizing reading strategies to engage with and understand the material effectively? How about their time management skills? Have they created a sensible schedule for themselves—allocating sufficient time, dividing the reading into reasonable chunks, scheduling the reading when they are typically alert and energetic—so that completing the reading is achievable?

As you can see, keeping up with the pace and rigor of reading is a coaching agenda that when examined, can mean different things for different students. Based on the scenarios above, the coaching agenda could be potentially narrowed to one of these three topics: (1) improving analytical skills with literature, (2) trying out alternative reading strategies to optimize engagement and efficiency, or (3) designing a more effective reading schedule.

Each of the above three possible agendas would lead to distinct coaching sessions. With just a little investigation, the coach and student can zero in on the significant piece of the agenda, recalibrating the session in a direction most valuable to the student.

Another critical piece to setting the agenda is remembering that the agenda belongs to the student, not the coach. By encouraging students to identify what they want to work on, not what the coach believes they should work on, students practice self-determination, or actively engaging in and evaluating their academic and personal development (Field & Parker, 2016). Recall our definition of academic coaching (empowering students to set and take action on their goals; better understand their strengths, weaknesses, and thinking patterns; improve self-regulation and study strategies), and you can see the logical expectation for students to set their own agenda. How disempowering for a student to have no or limited input into which way to steer the conversation!

Some students will easily take to the idea that the agenda is theirs, can jump right into the conversation, and articulate what they'd like help with. Other students may need encouragement and guidance. For students accustomed to hierarchical relationships in educational settings, where the professional has authority, they might enter an academic coaching conversation expecting more of the same, thinking "my coach is the expert and will tell me what to do." When a coach senses reticence or passivity from the student, they need to explain the design of coaching and assure the student that their role is to support, not direct, their growth.

Applying this idea—that students determine the direction of the conversation—can be easier when they seek coaching voluntarily. Academic coaching that is required can complicate the dynamic between student and coach and can engender a sense of obligation from the student. It can often be more challenging for an academic coach to encourage a student to decide how to use their time in a session when the student is obliged to attend. Sometimes it can help when an academic coach simply acknowledges the circumstances: "I understand that you did not choose to schedule this meeting with me, but since you're here, let's make this as valuable as possible. What would be most helpful for *you*?"

Similarly, academic coaching models that follow a predetermined curriculum could further complicate the principle that students set the agenda. For example, some academic coaching programs might have students attend a series of sequenced sessions where the topics are set in advance. Session number one might focus on time management, followed by a session on taking notes in lectures, and then a session on exam preparation. Students can certainly benefit from these types of structured coaching models, but without a say in shaping the sessions, their opportunity to develop agency and self-determination is constrained.

PHASE TWO: SELF-REFLECT AND LEARN

Once the coach and student are clear on the agenda for the session, the next phase is self-reflect and learn. That is, the academic coach guides the student, primarily through open-ended questions, to reflect on the topic. When we ask students to reflect, we want them to consider why this particular topic is important to them, their vision of change around this topic, and strategies they may have already tried. By having the opportunity to reflect, the opportunity to learn arises naturally; students might discover new approaches, additional resources, underlying habits they want to change, and much more.

Let's continue with the example discussed in the previous section regarding the broad topic of keeping up with the pace and rigor of reading in the American Literature class, and let's assume that the academic coach and the student narrowed the topic down to designing an effective reading schedule. The academic coach could guide the student to look back to evaluate how they might have managed reading schedules in the past, and they could guide the student to evaluate the pros and cons of their current approach. They could also guide the student to visualize an ideal schedule. Consider these possible soundbites from the academic coach:

- "How have you handled heavy reading loads in the past?"
- "When in the past have you successfully kept up with the pace of reading, and why do you think it was working?"
- "What do you know about yourself as a reader? What patterns have you noticed? For example, do you have a sense about how long you can read with focus and comprehension before you start to fatigue or lose attention? Do you notice if your reading effectiveness depends on the time of day/location?"
- "Talk me through how you approached your reading assignments in the last week."
- "Looking back on this past week, what would you have done differently? What do you wish you'd known before tackling the reading?"
- "Paint a picture of an ideal reading session: what would need to be in place? Where would you need to be? How much reading would you reasonably take on? How would you need to feel?"
- "Imagine a week where you've kept up with the pace of reading. What would that feel like? How would that impact your overall state of being? How would that impact the rest of your classes?"

These are just a sampling of open-ended questions a coach might use to generate reflective thinking from the student. And by listening fully and staying curious, every response from the student helps lead the coach to another question. In other words, an academic coach doesn't just fire off a standard set of "reflection questions" and then passively listens to a student's replies. The back and forth between the academic coach and the student evolves organically because the coach responsively follows the student's lead.

Let's imagine how a conversation between an academic coach and a student named Alex might unfold, based on just one of the open-ended questions above. Remember, the agenda for the session has been narrowed down from keeping up with the pace and rigor of reading to designing an effective reading schedule.

COACH: When you think about what an effective reading schedule might look like for you, let's start by looking at this past week. What would you have done differently? What do you wish you'd known before tackling the reading?

ALEX: If I'd have known how hard the assignment was, I would have started much sooner.

COACH: So how did this play out?

ALEX: I started reading the day before class, and I stayed up much too late trying to understand it and write a forum post. Not only did I not finish, but I didn't have time to do homework for other classes.

COACH: So, you stayed up late, but you ended up being unprepared for your American Lit class and your others as well. How frustrating!

ALEX: I know! It's like I just can't figure out how to do school.

COACH: Well, but you said you wish you'd known in advance how hard the assignment was, so it sounds like you do have at least *one* idea about how to do school.

ALEX: What do you mean?

COACH: You implied that "doing school" might require some advance planning. What does that mean to you?

ALEX: I should spend time looking through my assignments well before I start them, so I know when to start them.

COACH: Okay, let's apply that to your American Lit class. What would be some of the factors you'd want to know about each assignment to help you know when to begin?

ALEX: I should definitely know the page count. But the type of reading is also an important factor in knowing when to begin.

COACH: What do you mean by "type of reading"?

ALEX: Some readings are actually pretty easy for me, so I can get through them okay, even if the assignment is long. But this past week we were assigned poetry, T.S. Eliot and a few others. I'm terrible with poetry. I just don't know how to read it.

COACH: What is your experience reading poetry?

ALEX: Not much.

COACH: Then that makes sense that you struggled to get through it. So, if you knew in advance that you had to tackle a genre of writing you're not comfortable with, how would starting sooner have helped you?

ALEX: I would have known to anticipate a challenge.

COACH: And then what?

ALEX: Well, expecting a challenge would allow me to prepare for a challenge.

COACH: Good to know a storm might be coming well before it arrives, right?!

ALEX: Yeah. And also, starting earlier would just give me more time to think, you know? Some of the poems don't make sense to me right away, but maybe if I sit with them for a while, I can start to understand them.

COACH: Yes, I agree. The poems might need to marinate until you can get a handle on them. As you hear yourself talk about designing an effective reading plan and what you could have done differently this past week, what are some takeaways so far?

ALEX: I shouldn't wait until the day before something is due to start it, especially with poetry.

COACH: Good. And what takeaways do you have about yourself as a reader of poetry?

ALEX: I'm basically a novice, so I'm going to need more time.

COACH: That's what I'm thinking, too. So, when designing a reading plan, you will need to take stock of whether you're a novice or more advanced with the genre. Does that sound accurate?

ALEX: Yeah, I think so.

With designing an effective reading schedule as the topic, an academic coach might be tempted to dive into the nitty gritty of scheduling, have Alex get out the syllabus and a calendar and start drafting a timetable to read ahead of due dates. But, by spending time in the self-reflect and learn phase of the coaching conversation, Alex was able to uncover an important aspect about their reading skills. Yes, Alex had already recognized that they ought to have started the poetry assignment earlier. The self-reflect and learn phase of the conversation, however, helped Alex pinpoint why starting earlier is particularly important when reading poetry, a low-confidence genre of literature for them. And these reflections inform how to design an effective reading schedule, as we'll see as we continue.

PHASE THREE: EXPLORE OPTIONS AND ACTIONS

Before we examine the next phase of the coaching conversation, let's review. Alex and their coach start the session by articulating and narrowing down the agenda in Phase One. In Phase Two, they reflect more deeply on the agenda to better understand possible underlying, driving factors.

Phase Three of the coaching conversation—explore options and actions—integrates the learning from Phase Two and envisions potential next steps that would serve to make progress on the agenda.

While the focus in self-reflect and learn leans toward evaluating past strategies/behaviors/approaches, exploring options and actions leans toward imagining possible actions going forward. Note the plural on actions. An academic coach is not trying to lead the student toward a one-and-only solution. Rather, the coach wants to help the student be generative and come up with several conceivable plans.

This is an important point worth emphasizing. Academic coaches want students to develop the habit of brainstorming more than one vision for a path forward. Practicing this way of thinking doesn't necessarily mean that all paths have equal merit or could be a good fit for the student. However, by generating a variety of options to consider and actions to take, the student learns to exercise creative problem-solving skills, and they practice expanding their perspectives. Ultimately, the hope is that by encouraging students to contemplate multiple approaches to progressing on goals, they avoid (or minimize) stuck moments. Like us, you're likely familiar with hopeless or helpless narratives from students (or from friends, family, and even yourself from time to time!) when exploring possible actions: "That idea will never work," "I've tried everything already," "I can't imagine ever improving." While these are legitimate and normal feelings, they don't inspire hope or creativity. When academic coaches encourage students to see as many ways forward as they can, they lay the groundwork for students to apply creative problem-solving to many aspects of their adult lives.

The goal, then, for this third phase of the coaching conversation is for the academic coach and the student to come up with a few different options and action plans. They don't need to commit to one yet (that's coming in Phase Four), but they simply start brainstorming and evaluating potential plans.

Let's return to our scenario between the academic coach and Alex regarding the reading in their American Literature class. The agenda of the session was narrowed to designing an effective reading plan, and through self-reflecting, Alex realized that reading poetry is the essence of the challenge in this class. The academic coach and Alex will now begin exploring strategies to address designing an effective reading plan for poetry.

COACH: Okay, now that we've identified poetry as an important factor to be aware of when designing an effective reading plan, any ideas come to mind as you consider a different approach?

ALEX: Besides starting poetry assignments earlier just to be safe?

COACH: Yes. If we go with the storm metaphor mentioned earlier, we agree that knowing a storm is enroute allows you to prepare ahead. If poetry is the metaphorical storm headed your way, how might you prepare? What would you do to prepare?

ALEX: I supposed I could proactively ask my instructor for help.

COACH: Good. What kind of help would you ask for?

ALEX: Maybe I could ask for suggested analyses that would help me understand the big picture of the assigned poems or the particular poets? And maybe I could ask about themes I should be aware of. This sort of thing.

COACH: Yes! Basically, you're saying that the instructor might highlight key ideas in advance. What else might you do to prepare for the poetry storm?

67

ALEX: I could work with someone else in my class. Maybe just get together to discuss and share ideas. They could tell me how they make sense of some of the poems, and I could do the same.

COACH: Really good idea. Sometimes getting a window into how someone else works through an issue (in this case, a poem) can open a new way of thinking. So, I think collaborating with a peer in the class could be beneficial. Any other ideas?

ALEX: There's always Google!

COACH: Yes, there's always Google! What would you use Google for?

ALEX: I suppose I could look up the poets and read a little about their lives, their influences. This sort of thing. And of course, I can read about specific poems. I wonder if I can find decent analyses or summaries of poems online.

COACH: That would be worth checking out. A simplified look at complicated text can give you an easier way to get started.

ALEX: Right. I could read a summary first to orient me before reading the poem.

COACH: Yes, considering the big picture of the poem helps you know what to look for before you dive into the details. Okay, let's review your ideas so far.

ALEX: Ask the professor for help, collaborate with a classmate, see what I can learn about the poet on Google, and look for summaries or analyses online.

COACH: Good! And also, making sure you set aside time in your calendar to start poetry assignments earlier than you have been.

ALEX: Oh, right. How early do you think?

COACH: Based on what you've experienced so far, when do you think you ought to begin poetry assignments?

ALEX: They are always due on Wednesdays, so I think I should start them on Mondays.

COACH: Okay, good. Remember, earlier you'd said that starting sooner would give the poems time to 'marinate' for a while. Do you think starting on Monday leaves enough time for 'marinating'? You'll be just starting a new week of classes and all that comes with that.

ALEX: Maybe I should start on Sunday just to be safe since I have other classes to consider as I start the week.

As the sample dialogue above illustrates, Phase Three of the coaching conversation—exploring options and actions—is a time to lay ideas on the table. The academic coach and Alex collaborate in generating ideas, though ideally, the student begins the process, and the coach jumps in when needed. Indeed, academic coaches often have expertise to share—and if a student is upset or floundering or even shy, it's important for a coach to step in and suggest a strategy. Academic coaching should not be frustrating or anxiety-provoking for a student, and academic coaches should never withhold clearly needed information. However, starting this third phase of the session with the students' ideas is valuable because it keeps the students in the driver's seat of the conversation, and it also allows the coach to observe how students naturally approach various issues.

Another important element of exploring options and actions is to consider ideas that a student might not necessarily try. Why invest any effort into an idea that ultimately won't be utilized? The simple practice of exploring options— even those that may not be a good fit—can serve to broaden students' overall outlook. When students feel stuck and can only conceive of one or two possible options to try, an academic coach might ask them to imagine how a friend might approach their situation. Or if not a friend, someone they don't know but admire. Or a historical figure. Or a fictional character. The point is the act of embodying a different perspective while attempting to generate ideas can be a subtle but powerful tool in developing flexible, creative problem-solving skills (Kimsey-House et al., 2018). In the long run, an academic coach wants students to recognize that there are often many ways to achieve a goal.

PHASE FOUR: DESIGN AND COMMIT TO PLANS

We've arrived at the final phase of the academic coaching conversation where the academic coach and the student create a detailed plan that the student then commits to trying. They are no longer coming up with possible strategies; instead, they select one strategy to flesh out. Focusing on the selected strategy, the coach works with the student to create a concrete set of next steps that the student feels motivated by and invested in. By the close of the session, the student should have a very clear vision about how they will execute the plan, and they should also have a sense of commitment to the plan.

During this final phase, the types of questions an academic coach asks are geared to help the student think through the nitty gritty of their plan. Here is a sampling of typical questions:

- "What might be your first step? And then the next step after that?"
- "What sort of reminders might you need to follow through with these ideas?"
- "What are possible challenges you might encounter with this plan?" followed by, "and how would you navigate these challenges?"
- "How will you stay accountable to this plan?"
- "How will you evaluate whether the plan is working, or if it needs to be modified?"
- "How confident do you feel that you will be able to follow this plan?" and "What could you do to increase your confidence?"

The questions are open-ended, and their focus is on the future. The academic coach wants students to visualize themselves implementing their plan in as much detail as possible, and in doing so, predict potential hiccups they might encounter. Practicing this sort of thinking can be very useful; students can discover that designing successful plans often relies on flexibility and the ability to anticipate challenges.

Let's examine how design and commit to plans might play out with Alex wanting to improve their skills engaging with poetry.

COACH: Okay, based on the ideas we've come up with thus far, what do you want to try?

ALEX: Well, besides starting my next assignment on Sunday, I think I want to see what resources are available online to help me understand the poem and learn about the poet.

COACH: Alright. Let's think this through in some detail. Picture yourself starting your poetry assignment on Sunday. How would you begin?

ALEX: Umm, I guess I could read the poems first, and then search for online resources. Or do you think it would be better to find and read the resources first?

COACH: Both options have merit. Given your experience in the class thus far, what do you think makes the best sense for you?

ALEX: In the spirit of hoping to improve, I'll try reading the poems first; maybe something will sink in! Then I'll look for additional resources.

COACH: And how will you decide if a resource is a good fit for you?

ALEX: I'll use the assignment as a guide. If I'm clear on what I'm supposed to write about, I can skim potential resources to see if they will address the assignment.

COACH: So far, your plan is to give the poems a first read through to see what you might glean on your own, and then you'll look for resources to expand your understanding. And this is what you'll do on Sunday, correct?

ALEX: Yes.

COACH: Would it be helpful if you put a limit on the number of resources you use?

ALEX: Good idea. I can see myself looking up more resources than I would need to help me with the assignment. It would be my excuse to delay writing! I'll only allow myself three resources.

COACH: Good to know about yourself! And besides reading no more than three resources, what else would you do with them?

ALEX: I'd probably underline or annotate key parts. And then cross-reference the key parts with the poems—underlining and annotating the relevant sections in the poems.

COACH: I like this plan so far! Really good idea to toggle back and forth between the resource and the actual poem to find connections. What would be your next step?

ALEX: Depending on the poems, I'll probably read them a couple more times after getting what I can from the resources. Then, I'll look over the assignment and see if I have any initial ideas. Probably jot down a few notes. And that's all I want to do on Sunday.

COACH: I'm glad you're going to review the assignment on this first day as well. That should be helpful in formulating ideas. So, it sounds like you're saying Sunday is when you'll take an initial pass at the poems, use resources to help you better understand them, and make sure you are clear on what the assignment is asking of you, correct?

ALEX: Yes. That will be enough for Sunday. Maybe sleeping on it will make a difference in making sense of the poems.

COACH: I agree. What's next?

ALEX: I have a long break between classes on Monday afternoon, so that'll be a good window to start drafting my written response to the assignment. I'll have my notes from Sunday, which will already be much more than I've had when writing previous assignments.

COACH: Great! You've got every reason to believe the writing should be a little easier because of the prep you will have done on Sunday. If something does become a challenge, however, what might that be, and how might you respond?

ALEX: I'm often sleepy in the afternoon, especially if I stay up late the night before. I shouldn't assume I can be productive between classes on Monday.

COACH: Should you have a backup plan in case you're tired?

ALEX: Yeah. Maybe I'll make sure I get to bed by midnight on Sunday. I could also have a cup of coffee on Monday afternoon for a boost of energy.

COACH: Okay, good. A pre-determined bedtime on Sunday, and a cup of coffee as you start drafting your response on Monday.

ALEX: And then assuming I'm able to write a decent draft, I'll still have Tuesday to finalize and finish.

COACH: What might you do, exactly, when finalizing your response?

ALEX: I'd make sure that what I've written makes sense and answers the prompt, and I'd make sure that the actual writing is clear and free of grammar errors. I like reading my drafts aloud because I often catch mistakes better when I hear them.

COACH: Reading aloud is a great strategy to check writing. If you do discover when rereading your draft that something doesn't make sense, what could you do?

ALEX: I guess I'd go back to my notes or the poems for clarification. Or inspiration.

COACH: This all sounds good. Why don't you summarize the entire plan and make sure you like it?

71

ALEX: Sunday I'll read the poems and locate no more than three resources that might provide analysis of the poems or information about the poet. I'll annotate and take notes while reading. On Monday afternoon I'll start drafting a response to the assignment, using my notes as an aid. And on Tuesday, I'll reread my draft and clean it up so that I can submit it on Wednesday.

COACH: How does that seem to you?

ALEX: Pretty good! It's a much more organized approach to poetry assignments compared to what I've tried so far.

COACH: I agree. How confident are you about sticking to this plan?

ALEX: Very. Because I'm going to share it with my roommate. And she won't let me wiggle out of it.

COACH: Oh! Built in accountability. Super!

ALEX: Yes, we often make agreements with each other about finishing our homework. Very helpful for us both.

COACH: Well, this all sounds great. I'm confident the plan should make your poetry assignments a little less fraught. I can't wait to hear how it goes.

As the above dialogue illustrates, the academic coach uses specific, future-focused questions to collaborate with Alex in designing a set of clear next steps. The coach also engages Alex in such a way that gives them a sense of ownership to the plan. By the time students finish their coaching session, they ought to be ready, and perhaps even eager, to put their plan into action.

WRAPPING UP

One final but important note. Though the goal in Phase Four is to design a well-thought-out plan that students can reasonably implement, we also want to convey the message that the goal is for students to make progress, not to achieve perfection. In many ways, progress is the heart of academic coaching. Rarely are plans flawlessly executed because of the many variables that might intervene. Perhaps an instructor in another class assigned something at the last minute that messed up the students' envisioned study schedule. Or maybe a friend convinced the student to join them on an impromptu run. Or possibly the student's favorite study spot in the library was taken, and they lost time finding a suitable replacement seat. Through coaching, we want students to be able to make conscious decisions when faced with a conflict ("Should I go for a run with my friend now, or should I stick to my original plan?"), and to be able to adapt their plans as needed ("How will I make room for this last-minute assignment my instructor gave me?"). These self-directed questions and subsequent decisions are hallmarks of self-regulated learning (Seli & Dembo, 2020; Winne & Hadwin, 1998; Zimmerman, 2002).

We never want students to think that they failed if they needed to adapt their plan. Also, we never want students to think that they are failures if they were unable to implement their plan at all. Instead, we want students to engage with their learning process, identify the factors that got in their way, and consider how to readjust. Remember, challenges are opportunities for growth!

REFERENCES

Field, S., & Parker, D. (2016). *Becoming self-determined: Creating thoughtful learners in a standards-driven, admissions-frenzied culture.* Association on Higher Education and Disability.

Kimsey-House, H., Kimsey-House, K., Sandahl, P., & Whitworth, L. (2018). *Co-Active Coaching: The proven framework for transformative conversations at work and life* (4th ed.). Nicholas Brealey Publishing.

Seli, H., & Dembo, M. H. (2020). *Motivation and learning strategies for college success: A focus on self-regulated learning* (6th ed.). Routledge.

Winne, P. H., & Hadwin, A. E. (1998). Studying as self-regulated learning. In D. J. Hacker, J. Dunlosky, & A. C. Graesser (Eds.), *Metacognition in educational theory and practice* (pp. 277–304). Routledge.

Zimmerman, B. J. (2002). Becoming a self-regulated learner: An overview. *Theory Into Practice, 41*(2), 64–70. https://doi.org/10.1207/s15430421tip4102_2

Chapter 7

Expanded Skills

Academic coaching is powerful, adaptable, and expansive. To those new to academic coaching, it might seem like asking open-ended questions, listening fully, and then asking more open-ended questions constitutes the sum of academic coaching. However, we offer the fundamental tools as the foundation from which to build on. The central elements of academic coaching are always there, present and alive, in working with students. Yet, there are many times when other skills, strategies, and approaches may be helpful in advancing the goals and interests of the student.

In this chapter, we present and discuss ten expanded skills in academic coaching. We learned these skills through our coaching training and certification with CTI (Kimsey-House et al., 2018) and then worked on applying them within a higher education context. Each expanded skill includes a definition, a conversation sample of what it might sound like in an academic coaching appointment, and then a more detailed discussion.

ACKNOWLEDGMENT

Acknowledgment (Kimsey-House et al., 2018, pp. 53–55). *Acknowledge growth, effort, and achievement. "Do you see how well you handled that (challenging situation)?"*

Academic coaching consists of people working together to help identify and ultimately accomplish a student's academic goals. This is inherently interpersonal work. Connecting back to the definition, academic coaching is a "collaborative and trusting relationship." One of the things we can do as coaches is to see and acknowledge student growth, initiative, bravery, and more.

Acknowledgment can come in a variety of forms, but some standard constructions exist. As the example at the beginning of this section shows, there's a version of "Do you see…." Alternatively, this form of acknowledgment can be reformulated to emphasize what the coach observes, "I see how you…"

Acknowledgment tends to be more powerful when it includes specifics about what the student accomplished and the traits exemplified. While saying

DOI: 10.4324/9781003291879-9

something like, "I see all of the good work you've been doing" is perfectly fine, expanding on that acknowledgment to include specifics makes it more powerful. "I see the creativity that you used in adapting your study plan."

For some students it can be a challenge to accept and internalize accomplishments. Students may focus with precision on any small thing that has gone wrong or is suboptimal while concurrently glossing over accomplishments, even major ones. Acknowledgment is a method of carving out space and identifying, naming, and celebrating accomplishments.

While this chapter highlights and details ten expanded coaching skills, we fully recognize that there are many more skills and tools available. One related to acknowledgment is witnessing (Kimsey-House et al., 2018, p. 210). One of the great gifts of coaching is the long-term working relationships that form between coach and student. Witnessing is like acknowledgment but with the added benefit of an extensive interpersonal history. One gratifying aspect of academic coaching is to witness the growth and development of students over time. However, it is perhaps even more powerful to share that witnessing with students.

Academic coaches share observations like,

I remember when I met you during your first year at college and you kept on saying 'I want to be one of those students who has their stuff together.' And now look, you're turning in assignments days before they're due. I see how hard you've worked. I see how much progress you've made. I'm impressed with how far you've come.

CHAMPION

Champion (Kimsey-House et al., 2018, pp. 125–126) *Stand up for students when they doubt their abilities. "Remember how you passed the first test when you thought you'd failed? You're just as prepared for this test."*

Champion is closely related to acknowledgment as an academic coaching skill. What makes championing different is that this skill is used when students doubt their abilities. When championing, we stand up for students when they might not be standing up for themselves. In this regard, championing is related to the fundamental belief that students are "naturally creative, resourceful and whole" (Kimsey-House et al., 2018), they are not broken and don't need to be fixed. A student might not feel whole in a particular moment, but we as coaches hold them as a whole.

When championing a student, we rely on data and experience. Championing is not simply cheerleading. Telling a student, "You can do this!" especially if we don't know the student well can come off as hollow or inauthentic. We ground the championing in facts. Coaches can say, "Remember last semester when you had three exams in two days? I know you have the ability to navigate a tough academic stretch." Even if meeting with a newer student, there may be opportunities to champion. For example, we can underscore their agency in coming to academic coaching. "I hear that you feel discouraged and unmotivated. But you're here right now working on this. That's a sign a motivation to me."

ARTICULATION

Articulation (Kimsey-House et al., 2018, pp. 50–51). *Tell the student what you understand about the issue and what you see them doing. "I'm hearing you say that you're frustrated."*

Articulation is closely related to the fundamental academic coaching tool of listening fully. In articulation we take what we hear and see and then say it aloud, sharing it with the student. The process of articulation has many benefits. As with listening fully, Articulation demonstrates presence and connection with a student. These skills help develop rapport, build trust, and support collaborative work.

One aspect of academic coaching is serving as a kind of mirror to students. We catch things that we see or hear from a student and then hold them back up. Articulation is a method of verbalizing what we are seeing or hearing. That verbalization offers students the opportunity to see what others are perceiving as well as agreeing, disagreeing, or revising the statement. A coach might say, "So what I hear you saying is that your studying approach at the beginning of the semester was working and that things got off track in the past few weeks." Then a student might respond, clarifying for both them and the coach, "Well, it wasn't working great then, but it sure was better than it is now."

As a coaching conversation moves forward, a skill like articulation helps provide greater clarity and deepen understanding. Articulation is a skill that helps get a coach and student on the same page. By sharing what we are seeing, hearing, and understanding about a situation, we demonstrate that we are working collaboratively with students as well as providing them an opportunity to reflect on these observations.

ASK PERMISSION

Ask permission (Kimsey-House et al., 2018, pp. 123–124). *Get permission from the student to address an issue, make a suggestion, and/or share an observation. "May I share an observation?"*

As higher education professional we possess a lot of expertise and experience. We possess educational degrees, years of work, and tremendous knowledge. One misconception of this model of academic coaching is that everything needs to come from the student and that we are never supposed to offer our opinions or share our experience. Not true! While we want to start with the student's ideas and experiences, there will be times when in our professional opinion it will benefit the student for us to make a suggestion, share an observation, or relay an experience.

One method for sharing this expertise and experience while remaining faithful to the academic coaching model is to ask permission. Asking permission allows the agency and decision-making to stay with the student. We can ask, "May I share an idea?" or "Would it be okay if I made a suggestion?" Students will usually reply in the affirmative, but occasionally they don't, and a few are surprised that a professional is asking for their permission. Academia is a fairly hierarchical environment, and in general, any approach, skill, or strategy that helps flatten that hierarchy during the collaborative process of academic coaching is beneficial.

There are many scenarios in which asking permission is helpful in advancing the academic coaching conversation. This expanded skill can be used to share an observation about something a coach notices. It can be used to make a suggestion. If we think that sharing a personal story or an example from our own lives may be beneficial to the student, we generally want to ask permission. Asking permission is often implemented in conjunction with other coaching tools such as intrude and request/challenge that will be discussed later in the chapter. To ask permission helps shift back and keep the student at the center of the academic coaching conversation.

BOTTOM LINE

Bottom line (Kimsey-House et al., 2018, pp. 124–125). *Help the student boil down the essence of the issue. "What is the most important piece here?"*

In academic coaching as in other areas within higher education, we work with a range of students. Some students meet with us with a laser focus on what they want to work on, whereas others might come into our offices without really knowing what we even do. However, for all of us there are times when narrowing is useful. That's what the skill of bottom lining is all about, getting to the heart of the matter.

Bottom line can happen in multiple ways. The skill can be applied to the first phase of the academic coaching conversation. A student might sit down and rattle off any number of topics and priorities. At this juncture, we can say, "Of all the things you mentioned, where is the most important place to start?" In this manner, the academic coaching appointment provides an opportunity to practice prioritizing. There may be several things that are important, but we can't do them all at once. "Of these priorities, which is the main priority?"

Bottom line can be used during other phases of the coaching conversation. There are times during self-reflect and learn, explore options and actions, and design and commit to plans when it is important to help the student determine what's at the heart of the issue. Bottom lining helps bring clarity, purpose, and direction to academic coaching. We often say that sometimes the most powerful questions are the simplest. In the case of this skill, you can get a lot out of asking, "What's the bottom line?"

HOLD THE FOCUS

Hold the focus (Kimsey-House et al., 2018, p. 206). *Guide the session to stay focused on the agenda set forth by the student. "You said the goal for this session was to make sure you were taking better breaks while studying. We've shifted to project planning. Would you like to return to the original topic or continue with planning your journalism project?"*

As examined in detail in Chapter 6 on the four phases of a coaching conversation, academic coaching has both structure and purpose. There are overarching goals of reflection and learning as well as a process of moving to action by the end of a session. We often use the word conversation to describe the process of academic coaching, but this isn't just any conversation; there's an overarching structure and flow. One of the professional responsibilities of the academic coach is to keep the conversation on track. We do this by holding the focus.

Holding the focus is about keeping the conversation centered on the agenda of the student. Or, stepping back a little, holding the focus means making sure the conversation has an agenda to begin with. Often, we are working with students that we have known for months or even years. There's a familiarity with these students, and it sometimes happens that the structure and purpose of academic coaching can fade a bit. "How's it going? How have things been?" And while these questions are certainly fine, normal, and even helpful, academic coaching is not just catching up. You may be noticing that the expanded skill of holding the focus is closely related to the fundamental tool of managing self. In these familiar conversations, we remind ourselves that students are here for a reason and that reason is to get academic coaching.

Once the agenda is set by the student, the academic coach helps the conversation stay focused on that agenda. That's not to say that the conversation needs to be inflexible. Conversations, after all, have a flow to them and do not proceed along exactly linear trajectories. But if we notice the conversation drifting off course for more than a brief interlude, it's our responsibility to help guide the academic coaching back. We can say, "I think we are getting a bit off track" or "So getting back to..."

One part of holding the focus can be checking in to see if the agenda should change based on the progression of a conversation. A student may come to academic coaching to work on strategies for preparing for tests and they proceed to talk about how to navigate the time after their last class ends for the day. In cases like these, we ask the student, "You initially said you wanted to focus on studying for your upcoming exam, but now we're discussing in detail afternoon time management. Should we return to exam prep, continue with time management, or discuss something else?"

REFRAME

Reframe (Kimsey-House et al., 2018, pp. 128–130). *Guide the student to discover another perspective. "You're saying that earning a B on the exam means you're not as smart as you thought you were. What other meanings can earning a B have?"*

Reframing is a powerful way of viewing things from another angle, to broaden one's perspective. Reframing is an important skill in academic coaching because it helps students shift their thinking and understanding. Even if they choose to stick with the original perspective, it can be helpful to know and acknowledge that other perspectives exist.

There are several approaches to reframing. Given the centrality of asking open-ended questions to academic coaching, the classic approach is to use open-ended questions to reframe. We could say, "What's another way of looking at this?" or "That's one perspective. What other perspectives are there?" A student might have gotten a C+ on a chemistry test, and they announce it is the worst grade they've ever received. In asking the student about another way of looking at it, they might say, "Well, the average grade on the test was a C+, so it's not like I'm doing way worse than my classmates." Or they might say, "I got a C+ but I didn't really study all that much. If I start studying earlier and more consistently, I know I can do better."

In asking students to reframe, another method is to ask what advice they would give a friend or what their friends would tell them. Many of us tend to be more reasonable and level-headed when giving advice to friends. If a student says, "I just can't do this." You can ask what they'd tell a friend in a similar situation. It's unlikely they would tell the friend, "You can't do this." We are big fans of believing that we all are deserving of the grace and advice that we give others.

Generally, academic coaches start by asking students to reframe a situation, but sometimes it is helpful for the coach to provide a reframe for the student. Our reframes can be coupled with the expanded skill of asking permission. "Would it be okay if I shared a different perspective?" There are even templates that can be used for reframing. "On the one hand.... but on the other hand...."

One of the benefits of academic coaching is to help students expand beyond a binary approach to thinking. "I'm a success or a failure." "I can be a doctor or nothing." "I'm going to do the project perfectly or not do it at all." It's important for all of us, including students, to be open to a variety of viewpoints or perspectives. A common saying is that one thing we always have control over is how we view things. Reframing is an excellent tool to expand perspectives.

INTRUDE

Intrude (Kimsey-House et al., 2018, pp. 69–71). *Interrupt the student or pause the conversation in order to get to the heart of the matter. "I'm going to stop us here because we're getting off track."*

For some it might seem counterintuitive to have intrude listed as one of the ten expanded academic coaching skills featured in this chapter. As academic coaches, after all, we work to empower students to take the lead in the coaching process. The student is the center of academic coaching. We listen fully, ask open-ended questions, and believe that students are the experts on their lives. Where within this framework could intruding fit in?

As with any other skill, approach, or strategy within academic coaching, intruding is only done on behalf of and in service of the student. Generally, we intrude not to share our own ideas but because of something the student previously identified. One common form of intruding is interrupting the conversation because it is getting off track. In this case, intruding intersects with and works on behalf of hold the focus. A student might have set the agenda on a challenging or stressful topic, such as getting caught back up in a class and needing to reach out to a professor about missing work. In such a situation, it can be easy and understandable for a student to begin talking about other topics that feel less stressful. In these moments, it's helpful to the student and the academic coach to take a pause or time out and get back on track.

Some students are very verbal and can talk for extensive periods of time without seeming to take a break. We can have students enter our offices and start talking before sitting down. While it is important to honor and respect students and their communication, coaching is not just any conversation but a structured conversation. An academic coach can intrude to help structure a conversation, whether at the beginning, in the middle, or at the end.

Intruding can also be useful for an academic coach when a student seems to be trapped in a negative or unhelpful thought pattern. One common pattern is a student complaining about a class, professor, friend, assignment, or any number of other academic situations. While it's typically fine and occasionally beneficial for a student to vent for a little while, coaching is all about doing something at some point. Intruding can be helpful in these situations to interrupt the negative pattern. An academic coach can intrude and then say something like, "This all sounds like a tough situation. What do you have control over? What can you do?"

REQUEST/CHALLENGE

Request/Challenge (Kimsey-House et al., 2018, pp. 104–108). *Request a specific action of a student which can be answered with a yes, no, or countered with an alternative* action. *"Since you're trying to figure out the best place to study, will you commit to studying in three different places this week for at least one hour each?"*

In academic coaching we want the decision-making to remain with the student. However, there may be times in which a student could use an outside push to help get them moving. Requests and challenges should always be done in service of the student and the decision to do them belongs to the student. To expand the range of possibilities and allow for additional student input, creativity, and personalization, an academic coach should present a request or challenge by assuring the student that they can say yes or no or make a counteroffer.

A request is an action that a coach believes will help the student make progress with their academic goals. Requests can be as straightforward as helping a student settle on a course of action in the design and commit to plans stage of an academic coaching conversation. If a student is having a hard time deciding what to do a coach could say, "I have a request. We discussed a bunch of reading strategies today. How about you pick one and try it out with your reading tonight?" or "You've said that it's important for you to get to know your psychology professor. How about committing to go to office hours this week?"

Another occurrence of requesting in academic coaching is when a student has been putting off or avoiding a certain task. Perhaps most frequent is a student needing to email a professor or connect with a campus resource. In these situations, we often make a request of students, "How about emailing them now?" Coaching is all about moving to action, and there's nothing prohibiting making actual progress during the appointments. Within academic coaching sessions, students might read emails, check grades, make appointments at other campus services, text friends to set up study dates, reserve study spaces, and more. Sometimes the most difficult things we do are not technically difficult but require courage. Approaching these moments with an academic coach can help make them easier to accomplish.

Challenging is a similar but bolder form of requesting. In challenging, the approach is to suggest something really difficult. A student typically counteroffers with something toned down or different from the original challenge. However, their counteroffer is still generally more than what they had been prepared to take on originally. If we are working with a student who would likely benefit from additional practice before their next Chemistry exams, we might offer a challenge of "Do ten practice problems every day for the two weeks leading up to the exam." A student might then come back with a counteroffer of five practice problems every other day. As mentioned at the beginning of this section, requests and challenges are most commonly used when students are stuck or not making much progress, and sometimes offering a bigger challenge is what's needed to move forward. Challenging, however, should be done with extra care and consideration because the last thing we want to do as academic coaches is to demotivate students or shut them down.

TAKE CHARGE

Take charge (Kimsey-House et al., 2018, pp. 96–97). *Choose the direction of coaching. "Let's focus on preparing for your exam tomorrow."*

Of the more assertive skills within the expanded skills framework, taking charge can seem antithetical to the core of the academic coaching model. Academic coaching, after all, is all about empowering students and their decision-making and increasing student agency. While it's a skill to be used with care and consideration, there are times when you may decide that it's in the student's best interest for you to be more assertive in setting the direction of coaching. Sometimes this occurs when there is an urgent deadline with substantial consequences for a student, such as getting things squared away with enrollment or needing to contact a professor about a missed exam. A student might find the situation uncomfortable and would rather discuss preparing for final exams three weeks in the future. A coach might take charge and say, "Let's first focus on contacting your professor about the missed exam."

There are times when students have trouble making decisions about what to focus on during a coaching session. A student might arrive without any topics in mind or with a multitude of topics. Sometimes the structure of academic coaching might feel unfamiliar. After all, for many students this might be the first time they've done something like academic coaching. In these situations a coach can take charge and pick a topic to start with or focus on. A coach might say, "Okay. Let's start with your classes. Let's take an inventory of all of the assignments and tests you have over the next two weeks." Taking charge can be a way to anchor a coaching conversation if it's floating around somewhat aimlessly.

WRAPPING UP

With these ten expanded skills, the world of academic coaching opens even more. Coaches can mix and match skills and use them strategically when working with students. As in other parts of the academic coaching model, some expanded skills will likely feel more comfortable and familiar to you than others. We encourage you to try out some of the less comfortable ones and experiment. When we espouse the belief that challenges are opportunities for growth, this is not some glib catchphrase but something we deeply believe. And there's no better way to embody a belief than by doing it ourselves.

Coaching skills don't stop here with these ten. We've already discussed some more skills in this chapter including witnessing. There may be other coaching skills that you find that you'd like to adapt and incorporate into your work. Books and articles on coaching, coaching trainings, conferences, and discussions with other coaches are all great places to gain ideas that you might find beneficial (Kennedy, 2017; Kimsey-House et al., 2018; O'Connor & Lages, 2007;

Quinn et al., 2000; Starr, 2021; van Nieuwerburgh, 2020; Whitmore, 2017). If a particular coaching skill does not appear in this chapter that by no means excludes it from being helpful.

With this discussion of the expanded coaching skills, we are concluding the academic coaching model. All the pieces form a powerful and flexible method of working with college students. Bringing it all together is the focus of the next chapter.

REFERENCES

Kennedy, M. R. T. (2017). *Coaching college students with executive function problems.* The Guilford Press.

Kimsey-House, H., Kimsey-House, K., Sandahl, P., & Whitworth, L. (2018). *Co-Active Coaching: The proven framework for transformative conversations at work and life* (4th ed.). Nicholas Brealey Publishing.

O'Connor, J., & Lages, A. (2007). *How coaching works: The essential guide to the history and practice of effective coaching.* A & C Black Publishers Ltd.

Quinn, P. O., Ratey, N., & Maitland, T. L. (2000). *Coaching college students with AD/HD: Issues and answers.* Advantage Books.

Starr, J. (2021). *The coaching manual: Your step-by-step guide to becoming a great coach* (5th ed.). Pearson.

van Nieuwerburgh, C. (2020). *An introduction to coaching skills: A practical guide* (3rd ed.). SAGE Publications Ltd.

Whitmore, J. (2017). *Coaching for performance: The principles and practice of coaching and leadership* (5th ed.). Nicholas Brealey Publishing.

Chapter 8

Bringing It All Together

We've now built an entire model of academic coaching. We started with our academic coaching definition, explored the fundamental beliefs, examined the fundamental tools an academic coach uses with college students, described a four-phase structure of an academic coaching conversation, and then brought in additional expanded skills into the model. Channeling the foundational tool of curiosity and the phase of self-reflect and learn, we'll revisit each of these components, connect them to each other, and then apply them to two extended case studies of coaching sessions. We start with the full academic coaching model.

ACADEMIC COACHING MODEL

Academic Coaching Definition

Coaching has sometimes been criticized because it can seem like it encompasses everything and nothing. However, academic coaching is a purposeful practice. Academic coaches have an overarching mission of using collaborative, interpersonal work to support students in their near-term and long-term academic growth and development. The word academic is important here. In academic coaching, we help students set, work toward, and achieve their academic goals while learning about their strengths and habits. We help students become even better students. One critical and almost revolutionary aspect of the practice is that students decide where and how they want to advance their learning.

Fundamental Beliefs

To facilitate academic coaching conversations, we find it crucial to embrace and embody a set of beliefs. At the center of academic coaching is the belief that students are inherently capable. They are not broken, and they don't need to be fixed. While it can be well-meaning to approach the work of academic support in terms of wanting to fix a situation and make things better, that method can be counterproductive. We approach academic coaching from a strengths-based

DOI: 10.4324/9781003291879-10

perspective, one in which we focus on potential and possibility. But this isn't a Pollyanna, rose-colored glasses form of academic support. We know that many students face extraordinary challenges, and we don't gloss over those tough times or minimize the very real difficulties students grapple with. We do firmly believe that even amid chaos and struggle that academic coaching is a human-centered practice, and the humans we work with are "naturally creative, resourceful, and whole" (Kimsey-House et al., 2018).

Fundamental Tools

Academic coaching is an active, collaborative process between a coach and a student. While academic coaching generally occurs while seated, a coach is constantly doing something. The fundamental tools work together to help college students move toward success as they define it. Asking open-ended questions is the centerpiece, but the other fundamental tools of listening fully, being curious, and managing self all come together to facilitate those open-ended questions that constitute the model's core. These tools are how a higher education professional turns the aims and sentiments of student centeredness, growth mindset, and strengths-based work into action.

Phases of a Coaching Conversation

The four phases of an academic coaching conversation provide a structured framework for how the coaching proceeds. The fundamental beliefs and tools ensure that the practice remains individualized even within a structured approach. Academic coaching aims to benefit students on multiple temporal fronts. We want the coaching to lead to long-term academic growth as students expand and refine their learning strategies, improve self-regulation, and increase their metacognitive awareness. Concurrently, most students come to academic coaching to make progress on short-term goals such as preparing for an upcoming exam. The self-reflect and learn phase gives students an opportunity to think creatively and constructively. And the last two phases, explore options and actions and design and commit to plans, allow students to leave with immediate next steps.

Expanded Skills

Although this academic coaching model has a definition, beliefs, tools, and structure, it is meant to be expansive and not restrictive. The expanded skills demonstrate how the academic coaching model can be adjusted, tailored, and molded to an individual person and situation. People new to academic coaching might initially think that the entire process involves asking open-ended questions and that a student eventually comes up with a solution themselves. Asking open-ended questions is critical to academic coaching, and students regularly come up with ingenious and creative approaches, but academic coaches are active participants in the collaborative process. The expanded skills, coupled with the fundamental beliefs, provide opportunities for a wider variety of approaches to collaboratively work with college students while staying true to the overall academic coaching framework.

ACADEMIC COACHING EXCERPTS

As part of bringing it all together, we now present two annotated excerpts from academic coaching appointments. While these excerpts are fictional, they are composites of appointments and students we've worked with over the years. Both excerpts illustrate common dilemmas faced by students. Whether coping with a difficulty that is academic, social, or emotional—to name but a few categories—the experience may not be comfortable or pleasant. Discussing these topics with an academic coach helps students better understand their situation, how they feel about it, and how they might take action.

Within these two coaching conversations, you'll see the academic coaching definition, foundational beliefs, fundamental tools, and expanded coaching skills come together which help students make progress in identifying and achieving their academic goals. These excerpts demonstrate an entire coaching conversation but in a distilled and abbreviated form. The coaching conversations are annotated, and we'll take breaks at times to examine the coaching in greater detail.

In the first excerpt, we meet Brandon, who is experiencing low motivation regarding his classes.

COACH: Great to see you, Brandon! It's been a few weeks since I last saw you. What would you like coaching on this afternoon? Where should we begin?

BRANDON: Well, I'm not sure. Things haven't been going so well. I'm feeling stuck.

COACH: Can you tell me more about feeling stuck?

BRANDON: Yeah, I have no motivation. I'm barely doing any work for my classes. I look at my books, and it's just like "blah." I used to be a good student and liked my classes. But I'm not feeling it right now.

COACH: Would motivation for classes be a good thing to start with today, then?

BRANDON: Yeah, I think that's the main thing for me right now.

COACH: How are classes going?

BRANDON: The classes are the classes. But for me, it's just "blah." I know I should do the work. In some ways, I even want to do some work. But then, it doesn't happen. "Blah."

COACH: Walk me through what happens. You're getting ready to study or do some work, then what happens?

BRANDON: What do you mean? I'm not sure I'm following you.

COACH: Think back to one of the last times you tried to do work. Where were you? What happened? What's going on?

BRANDON: Oh, okay. Last weekend. Yeah, it was Sunday evening. Sundays used to be a pretty good day for me to work. I got out my textbook. I even opened my laptop. Then I just sat there and stared at the screen for a few minutes. Then I started watching YouTube videos. After about two hours, I stopped watching videos. I made this appointment. And then I went out to eat with my friends.

At this point in the academic coaching conversation, the student's agenda has been established, with the coach helping identify a starting point for the coaching. After setting the agenda, the academic coach moves to self-reflect and learn, working on getting student to explore the relationship between motivation and classes. Getting a student to talk about being stuck can be challenging as it's sometimes difficult to talk extensively about things not happening. In this case, the coach is getting the student to paint a picture of what happens when they sit down to do work, seeing if talking through that process elicits any ideas or realizations for the student. Sensing that this narrative description might not yield too much information for the student, the coach decides to change directions slightly.

COACH: Out of curiosity, if you rate your motivation on a scale of 0 to 10, where 10 is "1000% motivated, can't wait to study" and 0 is "couldn't care less," what would you say?

BRANDON: I'm at a solid three.

COACH: A solid three? What does solid three mean?

BRANDON: I want to care about my classes. So I don't think my motivation will go lower than that. But it's hard to see it going higher, either. I'm stuck at three.

COACH: I hear that motivation is a challenge right now, but I would like to take a moment to say I appreciate you coming in here to meet with me this afternoon. This service is 100% voluntary. You don't have to be here. The fact that you're here, wanting to work on classes, demonstrates a level of motivation and dedication to your classes.

BRANDON: Thanks. I did almost cancel. But I'm here.

COACH: You're here. And sometimes being here and working on things is an accomplishment just by itself. So, what do you make of the low motivation for your classes?

BRANDON: Hmmm. I'm not sure. I guess I don't find them interesting. And these classes are for my major. I shouldn't be bored by the classes in my major. I thought I liked statistics, but everything is so theoretical right now.

COACH: You sound surprised by that. Can you elaborate?

BRANDON: Yeah, on paper the classes looked good. Or I thought they would be good. Or I thought they would help me get a job after graduation. And now we're halfway through the semester, and it's all just "blah." It took me forever to figure out my major, and I finally declared last semester. And now it feels like I'm in quicksand. I'm sinking slowly.

COACH: That doesn't sound too motivating.

BRANDON: It's not. But hey! Speaking of quicksand, have you ever played Pitfall? Like the video game from, what was it, 1984? It's super old. Ancient. Way, way before I was born. I'm a huge fan of retro video games, and I've been watching YouTube videos about games from the 1980s. Old school classics. I play them all the time on this emulator that my friend showed me online. Do you know the story about the game E.T.? Apparently, they made so many copies of the game that they needed to bury them in a desert somewhere. I don't know if it's true or not. Do you know? I should look into that some, maybe do some research on the....

COACH: I hate to jump in here. But we're getting off track.

BRANDON: Oh, sorry. But have you played Pitfall? If not, you should. The old school one. It's like Frogger in the jungle. You might have played it growing up?

In the self-reflect and learn phase, the conversation changed with the student offering more detailed thoughts when the coach asked about rating their motivation. Sometimes, asking for a specific number, percentage, or ranking can help ground the conversation (van Nieuwerburgh, 2020, p. 90). The coach took a moment to acknowledge the student's effort in coming to academic coaching even though they are feeling low motivation. The open-ended questions in this phase yielded an opportunity for the student to delve into the disconnect between their interests and the classes they're taking. The student's energy picks up and begins to diverge into a topic seemingly not part of the academic coaching conversation, so the coach intrudes to get back to the original topic. The coach self-manages and moves past the question about their own childhood. However, the coach notes the increase in enthusiasm and their curiosity leads to asking a question to keep that energy in the conversation.

COACH: It's interesting. I can't help but notice how excited you are talking about this Pitfall thing, and I contrast that with when you're talking about your classes. This might sound outlandish given your current level of motivation, but what do you think it would take to feel similarly to your classes to how you feel about Pitfall?

BRANDON: Huh?

COACH: I see your excitement when talking about Pitfall and these video games from the 1980s. How could you feel similarly about your classes and your major?

BRANDON: Oh. I got you. Hmmm.... Oh. Wow. You mean turn my quicksand major into my Pitfall major!

COACH: I'm not sure I'm following you. Tell me more about what you're thinking.

BRANDON: See I've been focusing so much on disliking my classes and about how my major is stupid. Like I'm not getting anywhere, just trying to avoid pitfalls. But what if I could major in Pitfall?

COACH: Do you mean major in video game design? I'm not an academic advisor, but I don't think that's offered at this university. But I guess there's an Independent Studies major?

BRANDON: No. Not video games. I don't want to code or design games. That would ruin the magic. But what if I found a major that excited me as much as old school video games do?

COACH: That sounds exciting. But before we move any further, I want to circle back to the beginning. We had discussed focusing on motivation for classes, and now we seem to be moving toward exploring for a, what did you call it, Pitfall major. What's the most helpful direction for us to head in?

BRANDON: I don't know. What do you think?

The questions about being as enthusiastic about classes as video games led the student to alter and narrow the topic. The coach didn't need to understand the particulars of what the student was talking about in terms of video games, but the important part was embracing and channeling that overall enthusiasm. Making sure they held the focus on the conversation, the coach checked back in with the student to confirm the agenda. The student then asked a common question, "What do you think?" The coach had many ideas but self-managing again, they redirect the conversation with another question intended to help explore options and actions.

COACH: Well, here's a question. Take a moment and think it through. What's a time you were in a class or doing work for a class where you really felt in the zone? Like time was just flying by?

BRANDON: Not this semester, that's for sure. Okay. Okay. Let me think. This was over a year ago, but I really enjoyed my world geographies class.

COACH: Tell me more about what interested you about the class.

BRANDON: I've always enjoyed cities, and we studied in detail all of these cities from around the world. I ended up staying up several evenings and just Googling different cities to learn more about global urbanization.

COACH: Doing extra research on your own time. That seems like a good sign to me.

BRANDON: Yeah, it was super interesting. But I just brushed it off. I mean, I didn't know geography was a major. What am I going to tell my parents? Are they just going to say I'm majoring in state capitals? I know there's a lot more to it than that, but I really want to avoid hearing them sit there and tell me about how this college education is so expensive and....

COACH: Hold on. Hold on. You don't need to decide on a major this second. We're just doing some initial brainstorming.

BRANDON: My bad. I keep thinking back to that evening before I went to college when they sat me down and lectured me about being more responsible with my choices.

COACH: Of course. And I'm sure there are many things to consider. But we're just getting ideas out on the table. We don't need to slice and dice them just right now. Here's another question: have you heard any friends talking about classes they enjoy?

BRANDON: Well, I do have some friends who have taken public health classes. Some of them sound alright, especially the ones related to more global issues. That could be cool. I haven't taken any of them because I'm stuck in these quicksand classes.

COACH: What did your friends say about them?

BRANDON: I don't remember too much. What stood out is that they were hyped about the classes. Plus, I remember them talking about issues in different countries.

The coach in this section continued to manage self, focusing on exploring options and not delving too much into the student's relationship with their parents or analyzing the pros and cons of the ideas. The coach worked to get the student to generate ideas, and they come up with two in a relatively short amount of time. Mindful of the time, the coach moves to designing and committing to plans.

COACH: That sounds promising. We've generated two ideas here: the geography class and the public health classes, especially the ones oriented to global issues. I'm keeping an eye on the clock, and we only have a few minutes left. What are some next steps for you to keep all of this moving forward?

BRANDON: Well, I could go to academic advising. But I'm not sure that'll help me at this point. I'll talk to my friends who took those public health classes. I might also check out the global studies department to see what's going on there.

COACH: Let's get specific. What are you committing to doing in the next couple of days?

BRANDON: Okay. Okay. I'll talk with my friends this evening about their public health classes. I'll see them at dinner. And then directly after my classes end tomorrow afternoon, I'll poke around the global studies website to see what I can see.

COACH: Sounds like a plan. I see you already have an appointment scheduled for next week. So I'll be sure to check in on both of those goals then. I do have an additional request for something for you to try out. Do you mind if I share it with you? You can always say "yes," "no" or you can make a counteroffer.[1]

BRANDON: Sure thing. Couldn't hurt.

COACH: Over the next week, pay attention to when you are feeling excited about things and particularly motivated. You don't need to do anything else. Just notice those moments, what you're doing, and what's going on in general. How does that sound?

BRANDON: I can do that. I'm not sure I'll find anything, but I'll give it a shot.

COACH: Thanks for giving it a try. I look forward to hearing how things went with the discussion with your friends, the search around the global studies website, and moments during the week when you felt particularly motivated. I'm excited to see what comes next!

BRANDON: Sounds good! See you next week!

During this condensed academic coaching appointment, the coach embodied the fundamental beliefs and utilized the tools of asking open-ended questions, listening fully, being curious, and managing self. Circling back to the primary fundamental belief, the coach leaned into the student being "naturally creative." The coach heard and felt how excited the student was about their interests and research into video games and worked to continue channeling that energy into the conversation. They used expanded skills of holding the focus, articulating what's going on, acknowledging, intruding, and asking permission. There were many instances where managing self and holding the focus were used together. In this collaborative conversation, the coach focused squarely on the student and restrained from offering their own thoughts. The coach also asked the student to pay attention to when they were feeling motivated to help collect data for future appointments. In this way, the coach is offering a strategy to help the student build their self-awareness (Nilson, 2013).

In our next excerpt, we'll meet Mira who is navigating a stressful situation. She is facing the possibility of academic ineligibility due to poor grades. Unfortunately, this situation is common in higher education, and students like Mira need support to understand their options and to take steps to forge a sensible path for themselves.

Let's imagine Mira has scheduled an appointment to meet with a coach in an academic support department. She is approaching the end of her first year, and based on the grades she's earned thus far, she is concerned that her overall

G.P.A. might drop below the required level. Because she has been placed on academic probation after the first semester, she knows that if she doesn't pull up her grades, her next step might be academic ineligibility. Mira is upset and overwhelmed and wants guidance on how to best proceed.

MIRA: Things are really bad. I took two tests last week, one in math and one in psychology; I found out today that I failed them both.

COACH: Oh no. I'm sorry to hear this. How are you feeling?

MIRA: Terrible. Discouraged and disappointed in myself.

COACH: Yeah, I bet this is hard for you.

MIRA: I'm not even sure if I can pass either class at this point. I barely passed the first psychology midterm, and I already failed one math test this semester.

COACH: Sounds like this has been a hard semester for you all around.

MIRA: Actually, this has been another hard semester. I'm already on academic probation from the fall semester, and if my grades don't improve this semester, I'll become academically ineligible. My parents will be so angry with me. If I'm ineligible, I'll be stuck at home with them and feel like a failure. Actually, let's face it: I am a failure. What will I do for a job if I can't get an undergraduate degree? And how will I ever be able to live on my own if I can't support myself? What will I tell my friends if I'm ineligible and must leave? I'm so embarrassed and ashamed.

COACH: This is a very tough situation, and I can see how upset you are. The way you are feeling right now makes perfect sense. I want to assure you that you are not the first and only student to face possible ineligibility, which is indeed difficult.

MIRA: I just can't believe I might get kicked out of college, even though I graduated at the top of my high school class. What happened to me? Am I even the same person?

COACH: Yes, you're the same person, but college is a much different environment than high school. The good news is that you can learn strategies to adapt to all that's different in college: the demands of classes, your daily schedule, managing time and priorities, and more.

MIRA: Okay. I clearly don't know how to study, so I need to figure that out.

COACH: We can definitely include study strategies in our work together.

MIRA: But no sense in practicing study strategies if it turns out that I need to leave school, right? I wonder if I'd even be able to finish the semester and if my parents would get notified. What do you think?

COACH: I think you are juggling many concerns right now—math class, psychology class, your eligibility status, your parents, and a future job. That's a lot. Since our time is limited, can you bottom line the concern you want to focus on with me today? But know that we can address all these topics in future sessions.

MIRA: Umm, I guess I don't need to talk about a future job right now. But everything else seems really important. Maybe, something with my math and psychology classes?

COACH: Okay, how should we begin?

MIRA: I need to know what I'm going to do in case I'm headed toward ineligibility?

COACH: Right. I hope you will remain eligible. But preparing for any scenario and understanding your next steps would probably be helpful. And you can't prepare without sorting through what's happening in math and psychology.

The coach has used several coaching skills thus far. They have acknowledged Mira several times by affirming her feelings. The coach also helped to reframe Mira's current perspective about no longer being the same student she had been in high school, but rather, she's in a markedly different environment. As Mira cycled through her assorted worries, the coach asked her to bottom line so they could determine the session's focus. Eventually, Mira decided that focusing on her concerns in her math and psychology classes would be a good place to start. The coach managed self by choosing not to respond to each concern Mira brought up (her parents, her prospective work opportunities, etc.). The coach could have engaged with Mira about her worries, but they had a hunch Mira might be better served with a discussion focused on sorting through her status in math and psychology.

MIRA: Okay. One problem is I don't exactly know my current grade for either class, though neither is good. Even though I failed both math tests, I've done well on homework, and I still have the final exam to take.

COACH: Alright, let's start with math. How could you find out your current grade in math?

MIRA: I'm sure it's updated on Canvas [a popular Learning Management System used by many colleges and universities], but I'm afraid to log in and look.

COACH: Because?

MIRA: I'm afraid I'll discover that I truly am failing and won't be able to pass the class, even if I do well on the final.

COACH: I understand. Getting bad news can be difficult. But do you have all of the facts? I have a request: how about you log in to Canvas and get the facts about your current math grade?

MIRA: Um, okay. I guess I can do that.

COACH: Good, we'll know how to proceed once we have all the information. I know you're worried about your grade, so you'll take a big step by logging on to Canvas. When will you do it?

MIRA: I don't know. Probably this weekend. I need time to prepare mentally.

COACH: How confident are you that you will no longer feel nervous about seeing your grade in four days and that logging in to Canvas will be easy?

MIRA: Not very confident.

COACH: Yeah. Delaying could cause even more anxiety. I'd like to challenge you to open Canvas right now.

MIRA: Now?

COACH: Yes. Look up your grade right now so you know what you're dealing with. I'll be right here. You can share as much or as little with me as you'd like.

MIRA: What if I find out I am failing? Then I'll definitely be ineligible.

COACH: Maybe, but maybe not. We haven't yet talked about your possible grade in psychology, and you have grades in your other classes as well.

MIRA: I just can't bear the idea of academic ineligibility. Ugh.

COACH: Will you look up your math grade now?

MIRA: Okay.

The coach continues to use coaching skills as the session progresses, taking charge by beginning with talking about the math class. The coach also continued to acknowledge the uncomfortable feelings Mira was facing. Sensing that Mira's anxiety would continue to grow if she remained in the dark about her current grades, the coach requested that Mira log in to Canvas to see her grade. When Mira agreed to do so four days later, they challenged Mira to log in during the session so they could make concrete progress on the issue at hand.

Let's imagine that after logging into Canvas the student discovered that her math grade was just below passing. However, her homework grades are strong, and if she earns at least a C on the upcoming final exam, she could pass the class.

COACH: Okay, what do you think?

MIRA: My math grade is not great, but it's not as terrible as I thought it was. I mean, technically, I'm failing the class, but not by much. And I can potentially turn things around on the final exam.

COACH: Right! That's what I see, too. Though you didn't pass the first two tests, you weren't too far off because you're still within striking distance of passing.

MIRA: But it's not a great grade.

COACH: Maybe not. But for now, your priority is to get off academic probation, right?

MIRA: True.

COACH: Okay, what do you think your next steps are here?

MIRA: I need to figure out how to study for the final exam.

COACH: Yes, we should take a look at how you're currently studying and where we can make improvements. What else?

MIRA: I don't know. I guess if there *is* a path to pass my math class, I might not have to worry quite as much about academic probation.

COACH: I have an idea on that front. Would you mind if I make a suggestion?

MIRA: Sure.

COACH: Learning more about the logistics of academic probation/ineligibility would probably be a good idea. What do you think about meeting with your academic advisor to discuss your concerns? Now that you're close to finishing the year, a status update might be a good idea.

MIRA: Ugh.

COACH: What does the "ugh" mean?

MIRA: I just felt my anxiety grow again. What if my academic advisor tells me bad news?

COACH: I imagine your advisor will provide you with more information, such as steps students take to get off probation, the impact of academic probation on students transcripts, and options if they become ineligible. The information will ultimately help you know how to proceed in either scenario.

MIRA: Sounds scary.

COACH: Looking up your math grade in Canvas was scary, but you did it. You survived. Knowing the facts has made you feel better. Based on how you conquered your fear of seeing your math grade, I have confidence that you can talk to your advisor and be okay.

MIRA: Okay, thanks. Can I make another appointment to see you after talking with my advisor?

COACH: Of course!

As the conversation continues, the coach found opportunities to use more coaching skills, articulating the situation after Mira looked up her math grade. We can assume that the coach wants Mira to build on the momentum gained from their session and wants her to take more action. The coach, therefore, asked permission to suggest that Mira visit her academic advisor. Finally, after Mira expressed apprehension about such a visit, the coach championed her. Remember, to champion means to encourage someone by reminding them of the skills they have demonstrated. In this case, the coach pointed out to Mira that she could also talk to her academic advisor because she successfully looked up her math grade despite her fears.

WRAPPING UP

We've now completed detailing the academic coaching model, including seeing how the definition, fundamental beliefs, fundamental tools, four phases of a coaching conversation, and the expanded skills come together through two narrative case studies. With practice, academic coaches learn to be deft and versatile in using a range of coaching tools. The coaches from the two narratives illustrated the ability to meet each student where they were, and with curiosity and respect, coach them toward greater self-awareness and agency. Brandon benefited from his coach's skill in believing that Brandon's excitement about video games could be a key to unlock his motivation for his classes. Mira benefited from her coach's skill in taking charge with compassion to gently mobilize Mira into action. Both narratives also demonstrated that academic coaching is a holistic method of supporting individual students who have distinct dreams, concerns, and struggles. To adeptly coach one unique human after another, academic coaches benefit from having a well-stocked tool box that is grounded in a student-centered set of principles and beliefs. That is precisely what this academic coaching model provides.

Now that we've taken a thorough look at the chief elements of academic coaching, we'll spend the latter half of the book examining applications of its principles, skills, and structure to a variety of different contexts and frameworks.

NOTE

1 As discussed in Chapter 7, we draw the expanded academic coaching skills from our training, certification and published resources (Kimsey-House et al., 2018) with the Co-Active® Training Institute (CTI) and then apply them to the higher education context. For example, "yes," "no," or "counteroffer" is the CTI technique for requesting (Kimsey-House et al., 2018, pp. 208–209).

REFERENCES

Kimsey-House, H., Kimsey-House, K., Sandahl, P., & Whitworth, L. (2018). *Co-Active Coaching: The proven framework for transformative conversations at work and life* (4th ed.). Nicholas Brealey Publishing.

Nilson, L. B. (2013). *Creating self-regulated learners: Strategies to strengthen students' self-awareness and learning skills*. Stylus Publishing, LLC.

van Nieuwerburgh, C. (2020). *An introduction to coaching skills: A practical guide* (3rd ed.). SAGE Publications Ltd.

Part III

Applying Academic Coaching

Chapter 9

Common Topics

While the techniques and approaches detailed in this book can be applied to a wide variety of college settings, and there are several chapters dedicated to those contexts, we will now elaborate on common topics in academic coaching. The broad categories include time management, reading, and learning and study strategies. We also cover topics related to metacognition. Many of these categories, of course, overlap and are connected.

Please note that while this chapter includes a discussion of numerous learning and study strategies in relationship to academic coaching, this is by no means an exhaustive account. Academic coaches, other higher education professionals, and college students interested in more in-depth coverage of learning strategies would be well served by reading *Motivation and Learning Strategies for College Students* by Helena Seli and Myron Dembo, *A Mind for Numbers* by Barbara Oakley, and either *Teach Students How to Learn* or *Teach Yourself How to Learn* by Saundra McGuire among the many excellent books and resources currently available.

TIME MANAGEMENT

Time management is one of the most common topics in academic coaching. The reasons why time management is so prominent are numerous and varied. For many students, the transition to college requires more choice and decision-making about time than at any previous point in their lives. Frequently, students transition from having a daily routine and structure in high school to a college schedule that may be different every day of the week with generally less structure and accountability. In addition, the lack of parental figures typically means more freedom in day-to-day life, including what to do with time. This new-found expansion of freedom in making decisions about time can be challenging to navigate. In fact, while it is expected for students to encounter more difficult classes in college compared with high school, the transition in the structure and responsibility related to time can be even more challenging for some students.

Challenges with time management are by no means restricted to students new to college. Balancing competing priorities, making decisions about utilizing time effectively during the day, managing long-term projects, and combatting

DOI: 10.4324/9781003291879-12

procrastination all occur not just throughout college but also throughout life. One of the many gifts of academic coaching is that the skills, strategies, approaches, and learnings that students gain from this service are applicable years and even decades into the future. Time management has also been forwarded as an important element of self-regulated learning (Wolters et al., 2017; Wolters & Brady, 2021).

So how does academic coaching work in relationship to time management? Well, one good starting point is a classic open-ended question, "What does time management mean to you?" While much of the language used in describing learning and academics can be amorphous, time management can be even more unclear. When working with a student on time, it's essential to check assumptions at the door and delve into what they mean by time management.

If a student responds to "What does time management mean to you?" with "I want to use time better" or "I want to waste less time" that provides some information to you both. But without further curious questions and elaboration, misunderstandings about meaning can easily surface. The time management topic often turns into the proverbial peeling of the onion with yet another layer revealed as the discussion progresses.

If students want to explore the subject of time in general, one fruitful approach is to ask open-ended questions about how they use their time on a given day. "Walk me through a typical day." "How do you spend your afternoons?" The answers to these questions can be illuminating for the student. And surprising or not, some students simply reply that they have no idea where much of that time goes.

Sometimes these questions might be too abstract, and a student might have difficulty in recalling from memory what their days look like. A method to make time more tangible is to have a student, if they're interested, fill out a weekly calendar. Many students are fond of a weekly calendar in 60-minute blocks (UNC-Chapel Hill Learning Center, n.d.), sometimes referred to Google Calendar on a sheet of paper. Students can do this virtually, but many find utility in interacting with a physical object. A common method for using this type of worksheet is for the student to fill in all their hard obligations for each week: classes, work, clubs, etc. From there, coaches ask exploratory questions like, "What do you see?" or "What stands out to you?" Students answer with a variety of insights ranging from "There's a lot of free time space on the calendar" to "My days are really packed" to "I don't have any time to eat."

From the weekly calendar, some students choose to extend the planning and fill in times for studying or eating, or they target times to go to sleep or wake up. One of the foundational aspects of academic coaching is developing an action plan, a student trying it out, coming back to academic coaching, reassessing, and then moving forward. For some students filling out a weekly planner becomes an integral part of their strategic approach to being a college student.

100

While planning is inherently forward-looking, many students find it helpful to gather data about how they spend their days. Students often utilize the same sixty-minute weekly planners, but instead of mapping out what will happen in the future, they retrospectively fill out how they used their time. This method of information gathering is often most beneficial if done at the end of a day as remembering in detail more than a day at a time can be difficult. Coaches can channel the background of STEM students by saying, "You're a scientist. Let's collect some data!" As we state and restate throughout this book, coaching is all about moving to action, and the fourth phase of a coaching session is design and commit to plans. Sometimes, the primary action for a student is to gather more data, to closely examine what they are doing each day, and to pay greater attention to how they are approaching their time at college.

READING

For some students, questions in academic coaching seem like they have both no answer and an obvious answer. We ask, "How do you approach reading for this class?" Sometimes that elicits a confused look. "I'm not sure. I do the readings?" we might hear in reply. By using the same approach repeatedly without evaluation, students might not be considering the overall purpose of reading.

Within academic coaching conversations, college students often talk about "doing the reading." It's an evocative phrase. Doing the reading sounds like a chore to complete as quickly as possible like washing the dishes, mowing the lawn, or doing your taxes. However, unlike those activities where you end up with clean dishes or shorter grass, what does one have when they've "done the reading"? And that's because completing the reading in and of itself typically does not produce value. So, we ask students about purpose. "What do you think your professor wants you to gain from the reading?" Or "What's the purpose of doing the reading for this class?"

Academic coaches frequently talk about reading with a purpose. One question that often generates an interesting and helpful discussion is, "Readings can be used in different ways for different classes; how are the readings used in this class?" That kind of question can be followed up with "How do the readings connect with the other parts of the class, such as the lectures and assignments?" These may seem like leading questions, but they are not. When academic coaches ask the above questions, we are simply inferring that (a) the class has readings, (b) those readings serve some kind of purpose, and (c) those readings are likely connected to other parts of the class.

For some classes, the readings are directly tied to a student's performance and evaluation. In some classes, the readings track closely to the lectures; the in-class time might summarize and then expand on the readings. In other classes, the readings are used to generate and guide class discussion. And there are classes where the readings are almost supplementary, resources that students can use if they want to learn more about the subject or examine in more detail when writing a paper. Given the wide variety of ways readings are used, strategically assessing and implementing reading strategies would generally be more effective than always approaching each reading in the same manner.

Reading strategies are a useful topic to discuss how an academic coach can share study skills within the academic coaching framework. Through open-ended questions and reflection, a student may come up with a variety of interesting and potentially effective approaches to reading. However, we also know there are well-established and empirically supported reading strategies (Seli & Dembo, 2020).

We don't want to withhold useful information from students, so how can we share these and other study strategies while still embodying the spirit and principles of the academic coaching model? First, using the expanded skill of asking permission, we can ask if the student would like to learn more about them by saying something like, "Would you be interested in hearing about some reading strategies that many students find effective?" If the student agrees, we can then talk through a variety of reading strategies. Sharing several strategies is important because it conveys there are multiple approaches to reading (or whatever study skill topic you're covering) rather than potentially implying that there's one best way.

After sharing those strategies, a coach can then ask questions like, "Do any of these strategies appeal to you?" or "Which strategies do you think might be more or less effective for this class?" Typically, something will resonate with a student, like previewing or summarizing, and they'll incorporate this into their action plan. A coach could also make a request like, "How about you pick one of the strategies we discussed and apply it to one of your readings for the upcoming week?" For a student wanting to improve in an area, picking out something new to try and then doing it is likely more helpful than spending hours in search of the one "best" way.

STUDYING

Students frequently arrive to college without having developed extensive study strategies. From our experience, this is not to criticize students in any way. For many students in high school, completing classwork and doing homework is sufficient studying. High school classes are often very structured with more assignments due more frequently than at the university level. The need for independent studying along the way is minimized because there are more built-in checks and accountability structures. This is one of the reasons why in our academic coaching sessions, with very accomplished students, there's a common refrain of "I don't know how to study" or "I never learned how to study."

While students can come to academic coaching for a wide variety of reasons, and students by no means need to be struggling to seek coaching, one frequent scenario is with students whose usual way of approaching academics is no longer producing the results it once had. Some initial, exploratory questions in working with students on their studying include "How do you usually approach studying for your classes?" and "What does studying mean to you?"

When coaching students on the topic of studying and learning strategies, this can be an opportunity to share popular and evidence-based approaches, although we want to begin with students' ideas. Sometimes, students will say, "I don't know. That's why I'm here." One generally effective response to that sort of student reply is "I have some ideas, and I'm happy to share them. But I'm interested in hearing what you think first." In this way, we aren't withholding information from students but are keeping them as the primary driver of the conversation. We find that when assured we'll share some ideas, too, students feel more comfortable with generating initial ideas.

When sharing study and learning strategies it's helpful to talk through multiple approaches as described in the section about reading strategies. Two common and effective study strategies are self-testing and distributed practice. Self-testing comes in many forms including doing practice problems, teaching and explaining, using flash cards, drawing diagrams, and narrating problems. Self-testing involves recalling content from memory and can become even more powerful when that content then is applied and related to other situations, contexts, or topics from the class. Self-testing is a form of retrieval, one of the most powerful techniques for students to internalize information (Agarwal & Bain, 2019; Brown et al., 2014; Hartwig & Dunlosky, 2012; Lang, 2021; Weinstein et al., 2019). As discussed in the reading section, one way of keeping the spirit of the academic coach approach is to offer several ideas and then ask if any of them appeal to the student.

Distributed practice is the term for spreading studying out across time, making it the opposite of cramming. Distributed practice is also referred to as spaced practice and spaced repetition. Spacing out your studying can seem like the "eat your vegetables" of academic support. It's something that almost everyone agrees would be beneficial but it is generally easier said than done. As mentioned earlier, many students prioritize completing and turning in immediate upcoming assignments. If an exam is in a week or two, well, that can feel like a long way off. One approach in coaching a student about the potential benefits of distributed practice is to bring in evidence-based studies. Coaches can share with students that research shows that if two students study the same amount of time, but one student crams it all into the last minute and the other spaces it out that the latter student will be able to retain that information for longer (Dunlosky et al., 2013; Roediger III & Pyc, 2012). Retaining information is particularly helpful in classes that are cumulative or for subjects where the learning from one semester will be critical in the next semester.

Another approach to discussing distributed practice is bringing in a student's experience with sports, theatre, music, or any other performance-based activity. It is widely accepted that an athlete, actor, or musician needs regular practice and preparation ahead of a game or a performance. Students often make the connection that athletes, for example, would not begin practicing basketball a day or two before their big game.

The sports, theatre, and music parallels are also helpful when talking through ways to improve the performance-based elements of test taking. It's one thing to know the material, and it's another thing to be able to recall and apply the material in a performance setting. One of the reasons why tests produce anxiety among students is because they happen relatively infrequently. A technique that can be beneficial for students is to simulate the test taking environment and conditions. If doing homework and turning in assignments is akin to practices in sports, theatre, and music, then practice exams taken under exam-like conditions are akin to scrimmages and dress rehearsals. Students may take practice exams, whether provided by professors or made themselves, in a similar way. Some students might even go to the classroom where the exam will be held or take the practice exam with a ticking timer clock. By simulating and practicing in the test taking environment, students can get additional experience with the performative aspects of test taking prior to the exam.

Studying can also be discussed as a concrete structure. One popular and effective model is known as the study cycle. The study cycle consists of what a student does before, during, and then after class (Cook et al., 2013; McGuire & McGuire, 2015).

1. Preview
2. Attend class
3. Review
4. Study
5. Assess

When thinking about how students spend their academic time, some may divide most of it between doing the assigned work and attending class. Studying might only come along in the days before a test. For many students, it may not be common practice to review what happened in class directly afterward and then take steps to consolidate and internalize that information. If a student wants to improve their learning and studying, introducing them to the study cycle and asking open-ended questions around the steps to this concept could be beneficial. "What do you usually do right after class ends?" is an example of an academic coaching question about the study cycle.

The last part of the study cycle listed above, assessment, is critical to academic coaching and to developing metacognitively powered self-regulated learning.

If students aren't evaluating the effectiveness of their approaches to learning, it becomes that much more difficult to make improvements in these areas. Entire models exist that describe studying within the framework of self-regulated learning (Winne & Hadwin, 1998). A useful coaching question to support this part of the study cycle could be, "How will you know if your study strategy is effective?"

METACOGNITION

While it is unlikely that students will come to academic coaching to explicitly work on metacognition, many common academic coaching topics like studying, reading, note taking, and test taking are all directly related to metacognition. One of the overarching goals of academic coaching is to help students develop and improve their metacognitive processes, skills, and awareness which in turn improves the effectiveness of their ability to self-regulate their learning. Metacognition can be critical to a student's success in college (McGuire & McGuire, 2015, 2018). Metacognition is one's thinking about their thinking; within learning, it is particularly related to monitoring one's current thought processes about studying, being in class, test taking, and more.

Academic coaching questions often double as metacognitive questions. We ask questions like "When is it time to stop studying one section and move on to another one?" and "What are signs that your attention is beginning to flag?" and "How do you decide what to take notes on while reading?" In order to regulate one's learning, students must first be able to monitor and evaluate their current thinking. The action plans developed in the design and commit to plans phase around metacognition can be quite varied. Sometimes a student might design a plan to notice when their studying becomes less effective or what tends to distract them while writing.

Metacognitive monitoring can help counter or provide an alternative to evaluating one's studying solely in terms of time. We've all heard the adage about needing to spend three hours outside of class for every hour in class. Or maybe it's one hour for each credit? And we've all also heard students talk about how many hours they spent in the library, as if length of time spent within a building automatically correlates with achievement. In academic coaching, we can help students develop their abilities to assess the effectiveness of those hours in the library as they happen. Perhaps, they could elevate their studying through interleaving, which is switching between subjects (Brown et al., 2014; Oakley, 2014). Perhaps, they could notice when they reach a point of diminishing returns with the economics problem set and stop and do something else (like go for a walk outside). Perhaps, they could increase the percentage of time they spend in a library engaged in active learning strategies.

Improving one's metacognitive monitoring translates into students having more direct control over their learning and studying. Self-directed students are active not just in the approaches they use but in how they monitor what they're doing while learning. Academic coaches help students develop their metacognitive abilities by asking students metacognitive, open-ended questions. A recent study that we participated in suggested that academic coaching is connected with increased levels of metacognitive awareness in college students (Howlett et al., 2021).

WRAPPING UP

The range of student agendas related to college academics is great and varied. Within the landscape of potential academic coaching topics, those discussed in this chapter occur frequently. Because two of the goals of academic coaching are to empower students to improve their study skills and further develop their self-regulated learning skills, the popularity of these coaching topics is not surprising. As mentioned at the beginning of the chapter, our coverage of specific study skills and learning strategies is brief. If you'd like to learn more about them there's a rich literature on empirically-grounded approaches to learning, and some excellent resources are referenced in this chapter.

Although this chapter focuses on specific topics, it's important to recall one of the fundamental beliefs of academic coaching: we are coaching the student and not the problem or topic. We surely want students to make academic strides and achieve their academic goals. But academic coaching is a human-centered enterprise. At the end of the day, we are not working on reading, we are working with a person who has a goal of improving their reading effectiveness. The distinction may seem subtle, maybe even a bit pedantic, but in this model and these conversations, the student remains at the center.

REFERENCES

Agarwal, P. K., & Bain, P. M. (2019). *Powerful teaching: Unleash the science of learning*. Jossey-Bass.

Brown, P. C., Roediger III, H. L., & McDaniel, M. A. (2014). *Make it stick: The science of successful learning*. Harvard University Press.

Cook, E., Kennedy, E., & McGuire, S. Y. (2013). Effect of teaching metacognitive learning strategies on performance in general chemistry courses. *Journal of Chemical Education, 90*(8), 961–967. https://doi.org/10.1021/ed300686h

Dunlosky, J., Rawson, K. A., Marsh, E. J., Nathan, M. J., & Willingham, D. T. (2013). Improving students' learning with effective learning techniques: Promising directions from cognitive and educational psychology. *Psychological Science in the Public Interest, 14*(1), 4–58. https://doi.org/10.1177%2F1529100612453266

Hartwig, M. K., & Dunlosky, J. (2012). Study strategies of college students: Are self-testing and scheduling related to achievement? *Psychonomic Bulletin & Review, 19*(1), 126–134. https://doi.org/10.3758/s13423-011-0181-y

Howlett, M. A., McWilliams, M. A., Rademacher, K., O'Neill, J. C., Maitland, T. L., Abels, K., Demetriou, C., & Panter, A. T. (2021). Investigating the effects of academic coaching on college students' metacognition. *Innovative Higher Education*, 46(2), 189–204. https://doi.org/10.1007/s10755-020-09533-7

Lang, J. M. (2021). *Small teaching: Everyday lessons from the science of learning* (2nd ed.). Jossey-Bass.

McGuire, S. Y., & McGuire, S. (2015). *Teach students how to learn: Strategies you can incorporate into any course to improve student metacognition, study skills, and motivation.* Stylus Publishing.

McGuire, S. Y., & McGuire, S. (2018). *Teach yourself how to learn: Strategies you can use to ace any course at any level.* Stylus Publishing.

Oakley, B. (2014). *A mind for numbers: How to excel at math and science (even if you flunked algebra).* TarcherPerigee.

Roediger III, H. L., & Pyc, M. A. (2012). Inexpensive techniques to improve education: Applying cognitive psychology to enhance educational practice. *Journal of Applied Research in Memory and Cognition*, 1(4), 242–248. https://doi.org/10.1016/j.jarmac.2012.09.002

Seli, H., & Dembo, M. H. (2020). *Motivation and learning strategies for college success: A focus on self-regulated learning* (6th ed.). Routledge.

UNC-Chapel Hill Learning Center. (n.d.). *Weekly planner: 60 minute intervals.* Retrieved August 14, 2022, from https://learningcenter.unc.edu/tips-and-tools/weekly-planner-60-min/

Weinstein, Y., Sumeracki, M., & Caviglioli, O. (2019). *Understanding how we learn: A visual guide.* Routledge.

Winne, P. H., & Hadwin, A. E. (1998). Studying as self-regulated learning. In D. J. Hacker, J. Dunlosky, & A. C. Graesser (Eds.), *Metacognition in educational theory and practice* (pp. 277–304). Routledge.

Wolters, C. A., & Brady, A. C. (2021). College students' time management: A self-regulated learning perspective. *Educational Psychology Review*, 33(4), 1319–1351.

Wolters, C. A., Won, S., & Hussain, M. (2017). Examining the relations of time management and procrastination within a model of self-regulated learning. *Metacognition and Learning*, 12(3), 381–399.

Chapter 10

Faculty Applications

Emerging research suggests that academic coaching is an effective form of support for college students. While we firmly believe in the power of academic coaching, we realize that staff and faculty have multiple roles and approaches in supporting students. Not everyone can be an academic coach, and that's perfectly okay! But, perhaps, the most central experience for college students is taking classes. While professors have distinct roles and responsibilities, we think there's a lot that can be gained when faculty adopt and adapt elements of academic coaching in their classes and work with students.

One reason why academic coaching complements the classroom is that there has been increasing interest on behalf of faculty and universities to have course objectives to develop student metacognition, self-regulated learning, and critical thinking strategies. For many faculty, how you learn can become as important as what you learn. The focus on enhancing student learning goes beyond students enrolling in classes like science of learning and learning how to learn, though they have experienced tremendous growth and increased popularity. Faculty across colleges and universities are structuring classes and incorporating activities to elevate students' ability to regulate their learning, become more critical thinkers, and utilize metacognitive strategies.

Academic coaching also aligns with student-centered college teaching. As the authors of *What Inclusive Instructors Do* write,

> In student-centered learning, the role of the teacher is more of a guide or coach than strictly a deliverer of content, and with this the power and structure of learning shifts from the instructor to the students, who have an enhanced role in determining what and how they are going to learn, but also places the onus on the students to ensure they are holding up their end of the bargain.
>
> (Addy et al., 2021, p. 106)

In academic coaching, we aim to create collaborative, less-hierarchical relationships where the agency for decision-making and the responsibility for those decisions shift to the student.

DOI: 10.4324/9781003291879-13

Professors also have many one-on-one and small group interactions with students. If they ever existed, long gone are the days when professors solely taught classes and conducted research. Faculty are now involved in all sorts of projects, initiatives, and collaborations across campus. Academic coaching offers approaches that may support more effective interactions between faculty and students (Barkley, 2011; Howlett et al., 2021). While we will cover potential applications of academic coaching to the classroom environment later in this chapter, we'll begin with direct interpersonal interactions with students.

ONE-ON-ONE CONVERSATIONS WITH STUDENTS

Office Hours

Perhaps the most common form of one-on-one work between faculty and students occurs during office hours. Faculty may have concerns about applying the academic coaching model within the temporal constraints of office hours. Academic coaching conversations and appointments tend to be much longer than office hours, which can sometimes be as short as a few minutes. Understandably, professors might wonder about the possibility of following the entire academic coaching model, including all four phases of a coaching conversation, in such a narrow time frame.

A first possibility is to shrink the entire model and phases to fit into whatever time frame you have. While five minutes seems like a brief amount of time, the entire academic coaching model can be successfully applied in such circumstances. In these instances, it's more important than ever to channel the expanded skill of holding the focus while managing self.

There are also ways of truncating portions of the academic coaching model to streamline the process. One method is to have students enact some elements of the model on their own before office hours. The most straightforward way of doing this is by having students set the agenda beforehand. Sometimes a simple "please have the topic you'd like to discuss identified before the office hours timeslot" will suffice. However, a more reflective and iterative process could be modeled by asking students in advance to write down all the potential topics for office hours. Then a follow-up question could be, "Of all you wrote down, what's the most important topic you'd like to discuss in office hours?" Not only does this type of iterative, pre-appointment activity help make the time during office hours more efficient, but it also models and helps students practice the skill of prioritizing. While everything might seem important or even be important in some respects, there are always some things that are relatively more important than others. Prioritization is critical, and this is particularly true in the time-constrained setting of office hours.

The process from the preceding paragraph of helping students set the agenda prior to office hours can be implemented in an asynchronous format. Online forms can be used as well as paper worksheets. These pre-meeting activities can be expanded even farther to begin the self-reflect and learn phase. Classic academic coaching questions can be asked like, "What's been challenging about this topic?" or "What have you learned about this topic so far?" or "What makes this topic the priority for you today?" Some of these activities mirror those in active learning classroom environments which encourage students to do more of the thinking prior to the classroom so that the meeting can build on and advance those efforts.

One of the aspects of the academic coaching model is that portions of it can be selected and applied to different situations. Faculty and staff have found success in taking pertinent elements of the model and adopting and adapting it to their contexts (Howlett et al., 2021). Within the area of office hours, some professors will utilize one particular phase of the academic coaching model. A simple example is helping students develop an action plan with tangible next steps, generally within the SMART (Specific, Measurable, Action-oriented, Realistic, Timebound) goal framework, before departing office hours. "What are your next steps? What are you going to do? When? Where? How?" Contrast that approach to concluding office hours or an individual meeting with a student with "Everything good?" or "All set?" Elements of the academic coaching model can be used to connect the learning and discussion from office hours to a student's next steps outside of the classroom.

Helping students develop action plans is beneficial as it expands the reach and impact of the time spent during office hours. A student's learning does not begin and end during office hours. Given the often time-limited format of direct one-on-one faculty interaction with students, we want to make those instances as impactful as possible.

Mentoring

Faculty have a wide range of roles and responsibilities, with expectations and demands seeming to increase yearly. One central role for many faculty members involves mentoring students. Undergraduate students benefit greatly from these mentoring relationships, and they can become cornerstones of the college experience (Demetriou et al., 2017; Law et al., 2020).

Elements of the academic coaching model align well with faculty mentoring students. Mentoring relationships tend to last over months and years, complementing the iterative nature of academic coaching. Mentoring also, sometimes implicitly and sometimes explicitly, has the goal of long-term development. As in academic coaching, there are of course near-term goals and challenges, but there's also an emphasis on holistic growth. Faculty who utilize the academic coaching framework will ask students they mentor questions like, "What would you like to get out of this lab experience?" and "What interests you most in this topic?" and "How can I support your academic growth?"

The ongoing nature of faculty/student mentoring relationships matches well with the cyclical processes of the academic coaching model. Professors and students can collaboratively determine the next steps and identify specific actions to take. Then at subsequent meetings, the mentor can help unpack the learning.

Graduate Students

While the primary focus of this book is providing support to undergraduate students, this academic coaching model works well with graduate students. Many of the same strategies and approaches covered in the previous mentoring section also apply to graduate students. See Chapter 12 for even more discussion of academic coaching and graduate students.

In some ways, graduate students, especially PhD students who have finished their coursework, need even more support because they are entering territory unlike any other during their academic careers. While PhD students are smart, capable, and successful, they have largely achieved that success within the structured boundaries of coursework. Even larger projects like honors and master's theses are typically bounded within a time frame of a semester or two. Some PhD programs have structured dissertation phases, but in others, the process is long and uncertain. The dissertation can become a large, protracted, unstructured project where discerning forward progress is difficult.

The cyclical and iterative nature of the academic coaching model can help make and sustain forward progress and can make the overall process more concrete. A faculty meeting with a graduate student advisee can move beyond a conversation that ends with something like, "Does that all sound good?" to "What specific things are you going to do before we meet next?" It is more helpful to generate a set of tangible steps that will sustain forward progress. Sometimes the steps do not have to be particularly large or groundbreaking but can be a narrow and achievable goal like writing a paragraph within the week. If a graduate student builds momentum, the goal could increase to write one paragraph per day. While writing a daily paragraph might sound small, it's remarkable how much a person can produce when those days begin to add up. Much of this book was written using similar methods.

The structure and accountability of the academic coaching model can be particularly beneficial to graduate students. For many graduate students, the dissertation phase can be one of the most unstructured times of their lives. While having long stretches of time may look good on paper, in actuality these periods can be difficult to navigate. Using a coach approach, faculty advisors and mentors collaboratively work with graduate students to design structure and accountability. They can also agree to meet regularly with their students to aid them in making progress on their theses or dissertations. These meetings, incorporating elements of the academic coaching model, directly advance structure and accountability. There's structure because a meeting is on the books that a graduate student must attend. And there's accountability because if there has been an action plan developed at the conclusion of the previous meeting, the advisor and advisee can check in on the progress. One major aspect of academic coaching is breaking large projects down into smaller and smaller chunks. Dissertations and theses fit that description perfectly. It's one thing for a graduate student to have a goal of "write Chapter 2" and it's another thing to specify "read these two theoretical articles and write a paragraph on how they relate to your research by the time we meet next week."

An advisor utilizing elements of the academic coaching model can also underscore the importance of the graduate student process from matriculation to graduation. One thing that can get lost in the extensive time it takes to develop, research, and write up a study is that a central goal of the enterprise is for graduate students to experience a large-scale research process from start to finish. A graduate student may be fixated on what happens if their study produces a non-statistically significant result or how to overcome challenges they encounter during data collection, but an advisor can assist in reflecting on how this research experience can inform future endeavors. Faculty mentors and advisors can ask the following questions:

- "For your next study, what would you do differently? What would you do the same?"
- "What's been the most surprising or unexpected thing about this research process?"
- "Where did you spend more time than you should have? Where could you have allocated more time and effort?"

These questions can be asked in a non-judgmental manner with the stated emphasis on long-term growth. For graduate students heading in other directions than becoming tenure-track faculty members, the reflective questions can be equally as important.

- "What have you learned from the dissertation project that you can apply to future work efforts?"
- "In what contexts do you do your best work?"
- "What tends to hinder your progress and how can those things be countered or mitigated?"

ACTIVE LEARNING CLASSROOMS

One of the most significant trends of the past decades in higher education has been the transition to and emphasis on active learning environments. Extensive empirical research underscores the effectiveness of active learning environments and active pedagogies (Eddy & Hogan, 2014; Freeman et al., 2014; Haak et al., 2011; Sathy & Moore, 2020; Theobald et al., 2020). Active learning environments, which are highly structured and include opportunities for in-class practice, are also important components of creating inclusive classrooms and teaching (Hogan & Sathy, 2022; Sathy & Hogan, 2019). Active learning environments focus not just on what students are learning but how they are learning. They also have an overarching goal of developing students into more self-directed learners. The pedagogical and practical overlap between active learning environments and academic coaching is striking. Just as academic coaching helps students transition from passive to more active learners, many contemporary professors are structuring their classes around active learning.

At many universities, there's a frequently stated goal to have students take control of their learning. Active learning classrooms help facilitate student-centered and learner-centered teaching (Weimer, 2013). While there are numerous books and resources for faculty wanting to develop more active learning environments (Baepler et al., 2016; Beichner, 2014; Bruff, 2009; Cavanagh, 2019), this section focuses specifically on classroom approaches and strategies that incorporate elements of the academic coaching model. Here are some approaches faculty could implement to bring elements of academic coaching more directly into the classroom.

Metacognitive and Academic Self-Regulatory Questions

While professors are understandably very busy with time constraints on their one-on-one interactions with students, one way to incorporate elements of the academic coaching model is through classroom activities. Professors have many options available to support the development of undergraduate student metacognition (Ambrose et al., 2010; Cook et al., 2013; McGuire & McGuire, 2015). One method to promote student metacognition and self-regulated learning is to incorporate more open-ended questions as a classroom activity (Hoidn & Reusser, 2021). These questions could be asked to the class with students volunteering to share in discussion. Or students could be split up into pairs or small groups to consider the questions in a version of the classic think, pair, share activity.

Another way to incorporate asking more open-ended questions in the classroom is through asynchronous methods. Such questions could be included at the beginning or ending of a class period. These questions could be presented as something to think about or require written answers submitted either in real time or before the start of the next class. Open-ended questions could be incorporated into written check-ins. They could become part of exam reflections and review, a process that will be covered in greater detail in the next section of this chapter. Reflection, evaluation, and application questions can also be incorporated into asynchronous course modules, including those designed to teach self-regulated learning and study strategies (Bernacki et al., 2020). Incorporating asking open-ended questions into remote learning environments is covered in greater detail in Chapter 13.

These metacognitive and academic self-regulatory questions can become a helpful part of the first day of class. Incorporating questions about active learning in a first or second class could produce multiple benefits. For starters, featuring these types of questions communicates that in this class it's not just knowledge acquisition that's important but metacognition as well. Since open-ended questions help support self-directed learning, starting the semester in this manner also helps emphasize that this will be an active and not passive learning environment. Open-ended questions underscore an interest in the students and their thoughts. While classrooms are typically hierarchical spaces, these types of questions can signal the importance of student contributions. Open-ended questions at the beginning of the semester may also help model the learning strategy of predicting (Lang, 2021).

Open-ended questions could include:

- "How do you determine what you know well and what you know less well for this class?"
- "There's a lot of material in this class. How do you decide what's most important to focus on?"
- "What methods are you finding effective in learning this course's material? What methods are you finding less effective?"
- "How is learning the material for this class similar or different to other classes?"
- "What material in the class has been most challenging so far? Why?"
- "Where and when do you learn best for this class? What are the pros and cons of studying by yourself? Studying with others?"

Quizzes and Learning Checks

One common element of active learning classrooms is the inclusion of quizzes and other forms of learning checks during class time. As outlined in Chapter 2, monitoring performance has been identified as one of the core components of self-regulated learning (Seli & Dembo, 2020; Zimmerman & Risemberg, 1997). Quizzes and understanding checks in active learning environments are based on the learning strategy of self-testing (see Chapters 9 and 10). One of the classic and understandable phrases from traditional classrooms is something akin to "does this all make sense?" Many students respond by nodding, whether or not they understand the material. Quizzes and learning checks are ways for the professor and students to assess what they are understanding and where there might be gaps in knowledge. These learning checks help students see that it's not just about getting the right answer but that understanding how and why the answer is correct is often more important.

While incorporating quizzes and learning checks is nothing new in active learning environments, faculty can lean on elements of the academic coaching model to help students better understand why classes are structured in this way. Academic coaches frequently ask students questions like, "What does your professor want you to get out of this activity?" and "Why do you think the professor structured the course in this manner?" and "Why do your professors provide guided reading questions for this class?" Faculty can open a class for reflection on the process of activities. "What's the purpose of these quizzes and learning checks?" Even if students don't come up with it on their own, it's valuable knowledge that there is extensive empirical research showing that these activities improve learning. And, in fact, students can utilize similar methods on their own as they study for this and other classes.

Exam and Paper Review

When a student receives back an exam, assignment, or paper this is a wonderful opportunity for additional learning. Too frequently there's a quick check of the grade. If the grade is "good" students typically move on. If the grade isn't so good, sometimes there's more of an examination of where things went astray. But whatever the grade, many students might be tempted to just keep moving forward. And this tendency is understandable. Students are busy and the assignment, exam, or paper is now in the past. There's nothing more that can be done, right?

There are still extensive learning opportunities for students. Faculty can help spur additional reflection and learning by making post-exam and paper activities official parts of their classes. And while many classes feature retrospective test reviews, they less frequently feature reflections of self-regulatory learning processes. However, post-exam reflections, both written and conversational, can be powerful activities in helping students develop metacognitive processes (Medina et al., 2017; Raković et al., 2022).

Faculty could incorporate open-ended questions within exam and paper reviews. Some potential questions for these reviews include:

- "How did you prepare for the exam?" or "How did you approach writing the paper?"
- "In your assessment, what went well in your preparations? What could have been improved?"
- "Were there aspects of your preparation where you dedicated more time than you should have? Were there parts of your preparation where you could have benefited from dedicating more time?"

- "How well did your exam preparations match up with what was covered on the exam?"
- "How would you describe your studying or paper writing process to someone else?"
- "The next time you study for an exam or write a paper, what will you keep the same?"
- "What will you do differently?"

An exam, assignment, or paper is just one part of a student's long academic career. These are not students' first forays into assessments nor their last. While professors, departments, and universities are understandably focused on content acquisition and mastery, these retrospective assessments provide opportunities to help students better understand and develop their approaches to learning. Growing these self-regulatory and metacognitive skills benefits students not just in the short term, but later as they move on from college as lifelong learners.

WRAPPING UP

While academic coaching has emerged within a broader trend to support student learning outside of the classroom, there are numerous ways in which faculty may implement parts or all of the academic coaching model in their work with students. Professors, whether in classes, office hours, labs, or other settings frequently interact with college students, and we believe academic coaching approaches can help make those interactions more effective. In our research study that examined the impacts of academic coaching training on faculty and staff, the areas with the largest impact were on collaboration, asking open-ended questions, and creating an action plan (Howlett et al., 2021). As higher education increasingly emphasizes the importance of students becoming self-directed learners, the tools and approaches of academic coaching can help equip faculty to facilitate those abilities in their students.

REFERENCES

Addy, T. M., Dube, D., Mitchell, K. A., & SoRelle, M. E. (2021). *What inclusive instructors do: Principles and practices for excellence in college teaching.* Stylus Publishing.

Ambrose, S. A., Bridges, M. W., DiPietro, Mi., Lovett, M. C., & Norman, M. K. (2010). *How learning works: 7 research-based principles for smart teaching.* Jossey-Bass.

Baepler, P., Walker, J., Brooks, D. C., Saichaie, K., & Petersen, C. I. (2016). *A guide to teaching in the active learning classroom: History, research, and practice.* Stylus Publishing, LLC.

Barkley, A. (2011). Academic coaching for enhanced learning. *NACTA Journal, 55*(1), 76–81. https://www.jstor.org/stable/nactajournal.55.1.76

Beichner, R. J. (2014). History and evolution of active learning spaces. *New Directions for Teaching and Learning, 2014*(137), 9–16. https://doi.org/10.1002/tl.20081

Bernacki, M. L., Vosicka, L., & Utz, J. C. (2020). Can a brief, digital skill training intervention help undergraduates "learn to learn" and improve their STEM achievement? *Journal of Educational Psychology, 112*(4), 765–781. https://doi.org/10.1037/edu0000405

Bruff, D. (2009). *Teaching with classroom response systems: Creative active learning environments.* Jossey-Bass.

Cavanagh, S. R. (2019). How to make your teaching more engaging. *The Chronicle of Higher Education.* https://www.chronicle.com/article/how-to-make-your-teaching-more-engaging/

Cook, E., Kennedy, E., & McGuire, S. Y. (2013). Effect of teaching metacognitive learning strategies on performance in general chemistry courses. *Journal of Chemical Education, 90*(8), 961–967. https://doi.org/10.1021/ed300686h

Demetriou, C., Meece, J., Eaker-Rich, D., & Powell, C. (2017). The activities, roles, and relationships of successful first-generation college students. *Journal of College Student Development, 58*(1), 19–36. https://doi.org/10.1353/csd.2017.0001

Eddy, S. L., & Hogan, K. A. (2014). Getting under the hood: How and for whom does increasing course structure work? *CBE—Life Sciences Education, 13*(3), 453–468.

Freeman, S., Eddy, S. L., McDonough, M., Smith, M. K., Okoroafor, N., Jordt, H., & Wenderoth, M. P. (2014). Active learning increases student performance in science, engineering, and mathematics. *Proceedings of the National Academy of Sciences, 111*(23), 8410–8415.

Haak, D. C., HilleRisLambers, J., Pitre, E., & Freeman, S. (2011). Increased structure and active learning reduce the achievement gap in introductory biology. *Science, 332*(6034), 1213–1216. https://doi.org/10.1126/science.1204820

Hogan, K. A., & Sathy, V. (2022). *Inclusive teaching: Strategies for promoting equity in the college classroom.* West Virginia University Press.

Hoidn, S., & Reusser, K. (2021). Foundations of student-centered learning and teaching. In S. Hoidn & M. Klemencic (Eds.), *The Routledge international handbook of student-centered learning and teaching in higher education* (pp. 17–46). Routledge.

Howlett, M. A., McWilliams, M. A., Rademacher, K., Maitland, T. L., O'Neill, J. C., Abels, K., Demetriou, C., & Panter, A. (2021). An academic coaching training program for university professionals: A mixed methods examination. *Journal of Student Affairs Research and Practice, 58*(3), 335–349. https://doi.org/10.1080/19496591.2020.1784750

Lang, J. M. (2021). *Small teaching: Everyday lessons from the science of learning* (2nd ed.). Jossey-Bass.

Law, D. D., Hales, K., & Busenbark, D. (2020). Student success: A literature review of faculty to student mentoring. *Journal on Empowering Teaching Excellence, 4*(1), 6. https://doi.org/10.15142/38x2-n847

McGuire, S. Y., & McGuire, S. (2015). *Teach students how to learn: Strategies you can incorporate into any course to improve student metacognition, study skills, and motivation.* Stylus Publishing.

Medina, M. S., Castleberry, A. N., & Persky, A. M. (2017). Strategies for improving learner metacognition in health professional education. *American Journal of Pharmaceutical Education, 81*(4). https://doi.org/10.5688/ajpe81478

Raković, M., Bernacki, M. L., Greene, J. A., Plumley, R. D., Hogan, K. A., Gates, K. M., & Panter, A. T. (2022). Examining the critical role of evaluation and adaptation in self-regulated learning. *Contemporary Educational Psychology, 68*, 102027. https://doi.org/10.1016/j.cedpsych.2021.102027

Sathy, V., & Hogan, K. (2019, July 22). How to make your teaching more inclusive. *Chronicle of Higher Education.* https://www.chronicle.com/article/how-to-make-your-teaching-more-inclusive/

Sathy, V., & Moore, Q. (2020). Who benefits from the flipped classroom?: Quasi-experimental findings on student learning, engagement, course perceptions, and interest in statistics. In J. L. Rodgers (Ed.), *Teaching statistics and quantitative methods in the 21st century* (pp. 197–216). Routledge.

Seli, H., & Dembo, M. H. (2020). *Motivation and learning strategies for college success: A focus on self-regulated learning* (6th ed.). Routledge.

Theobald, E. J., Hill, M. J., Tran, E., Agrawal, S., Arroyo, E. N., Behling, S., Chambwe, N., Cintrón, D. L., Cooper, J. D., Dunster, G., & others. (2020). Active learning narrows achievement gaps for underrepresented students in undergraduate science, technology, engineering, and math. *Proceedings of the National Academy of Sciences, 117*(12), 6476–6483. https://doi.org/10.1073/pnas.1916903117

Weimer, M. (2013). *Learner-centered teaching: Five key changes to practice* (2nd ed.). Jossey-Bass.

Zimmerman, B. J., & Risemberg, R. (1997). Self-regulatory dimensions of academic learning and motivation. In G. D. Phye (Ed.), *Handbook of academic learning: Construction of knowledge* (pp. 105–125). Academic Press.

Chapter 11

Staff Applications

On a typical day on a college campus, students regularly interact with staff from various offices. In some contexts, students might have relatively limited individual contact with their faculty compared with conversations they have with staff in offices like academic support, academic advising, career services, accessibility services, and many of the departments housed in student affairs. College staff, therefore, play a vital role in contributing to the overall experience of students, and they can effectively utilize the academic coaching model to support and enrich their work with students.

Let's look at how staff in a variety of roles from different departments on a college campus can implement academic coaching skills, even in brief interactions with students. In many student interactions, staff may need to provide policy information, make referrals to other offices, or simply answer students' questions. Likewise, sometimes staff need to gather basic information from students in which open-ended, coaching-type questions are not helpful. Implementing a full academic coaching conversation as described thus far in the book is impractical and might even be unhelpful in these moments. For example, if a student wanders into the academic advising department asking to talk about feeling anxious and depressed, it might be inappropriate to launch into a series of open-ended questions. An extreme example of a terribly timed and insensitive coaching question could be: "I'm not a counselor, nor is anyone in this department, but can you imagine where on campus you might find one?" Ouch. Instead, a moment like the above is the time to clarify one's role as an academic advisor and assist in that capacity. But also, the advisor would want to warmly refer the student to the school's counseling services, make sure the student knows how to access these services, and guide them further if needed.

We should also note that depending on a professional's role in an office or department, student interactions vary in length and purpose. However, staff can still implement the coaching model in their unique contexts. Remembering the fundamental principles of academic coaching will be helpful, even in brief conversations:

- Collaborate with, instead of fixing the student; after all, they are "naturally creative, resourceful and whole" (Kimsey-House et al., 2018).
- While professionals have expertise, the student is the expert on their life.
- Because coaching is holistic, focus the conversation on the student, not on the particular problem or struggle the student faces.
- Invite the student to set the agenda for their time with you and assist in narrowing it down if necessary.
- Ask open-ended questions to help the student reflect.
- Provide necessary information when appropriate (as in the example about counseling services above).
- Aim to stay curious throughout your conversation, which will help thwart tendencies to jump into advice-giving, judgment, or assumption-making.
- Listen, listen, listen!
- Collaborate with the student in generating ideas, strategies, and possible plans.
- Help the student nail down a final plan.

Let's look at how to apply academic coaching in different university staff contexts.

ACADEMIC SUPPORT DEPARTMENTS

The academic coaching model described in this book was first developed for staff in academic support roles within a university learning center, and this method of working with students is an excellent fit for these types of professionals. In fact, Part 6 of the academic coaching definition reflects the origins of the model ("Academic coaching empowers students to learn effective study skills"). We have, thus far, provided many coaching examples based on scenarios where students might be working with a coach serving in an academic support department. Notably, academic support departments across campuses may lack uniformity regarding staff descriptions. Tutors, academic coaches, and academic advisors are titles often used interchangeably. Sometimes, tutors are renamed to academic coaches, though the ways they work with students remain unchanged.

When we discuss applying the academic coaching model in academic support departments, we include all professionals in these roles. Still, we differentiate an academic coach from a tutor in the following way: academic coaches support students on a broad range of academic issues, while tutors help students in academic matters related to a particular class or subject area.

Because we've looked at several examples in earlier chapters of professionals serving as academic coaches, let's look at how professionals serving as tutors could apply academic coaching principles and skills.

Traditional tutoring can tend to be directive. A tutor might diagnose the student's struggling issue and then direct them to or teach them the solutions. The tutor is in charge of the session, and the student is merely along for the ride. When using a coach approach, however, the tutor and student collaborate to discover where the student needs assistance, and then together they explore new techniques to gain greater clarity. The tutor wants the student to leave the session equipped to work independently and to have strategies in place if they get stuck.

Imagine a tutor is working with a student struggling with advanced grammar in their Spanish class. The tutor will rely on questions to help the student articulate what they do and do not understand about the grammar and to reflect on why it might be tripping them up. Questions that might help them know what's at the root of the why could include the following:

- "What's the most challenging part for you?"
- "What have you tried so far?"
- "What grammar guidelines could be essential to memorize?"
- "What resources (in addition to tutoring) are available to help you when stuck?"

The tutor would also want to see the student work through grammar exercises (as opposed to the student watching the tutor do the work) so that in uncertain moments, the tutor can ask helpful coaching questions:

- "Talk through your thinking right now."
- "What are your options here?"
- "How could you find clues about how to proceed?"
- "What if we look in your textbook together to review this particular procedure?"

At no point is the tutor simply directing the student to their next steps or even reteaching content. When using the principles of the academic coaching model, the tutor begins by engaging the student's own problem-solving and critical thinking skills. Often, good coaching questions will nudge a student toward developing independent learning skills—an essential skill in college. While it might be quicker to review or reteach pertinent grammar rules to the student, doing only that could deprive them of the opportunity to learn methods of getting unstuck on their own.

When tutors use a coach approach—relying primarily on collaboration and questions—the impact on the student will be broader and more enduring. And best practices in peer tutoring, which emphasize processes, strategies, and approaches to learning, share many similarities with academic coaching (Clemons et al., 2018; Lipsky, 2011; Saenz et al., 2021; Toms, 2010).

ACADEMIC ADVISING

The titles of academic advisors and academic coaches can also be used differently from one institution to the next. For this chapter, we define an academic advisor as someone whose responsibilities include helping students explore academic interests, assist with academic planning including choosing a major, and ensure that they meet graduation requirements.

When utilizing the academic coaching model, academic advisors have an excellent opportunity to help students start forging a path toward their academic interests and professional goals. They will also see students with varying levels of clarity about their plans. Some students might begin the first day of their first year confident that they will enter a pre-med path and no other course of study is even possible. Some might arrive at the halfway point of their time in college and decide they hate their declared business major and want to change it. Some might cautiously declare a major in the humanities as they aren't sure where it will take them, but they love humanities and cannot imagine studying anything else.

The second phase of the coaching conversation, self-reflect and learn, can be beneficial in scenarios like the above. Asking open-ended questions gives students the space to reflect on their skills, strengths, and dreams, allowing them to make measured and considered decisions about their future. Consider how the following questions encourage students to think critically about their choices:

- "Of all your classes this semester, which one(s) motivate you the most? The least? Can you explain why?"
- "Tell me about your desire to enter the pre-med track. What might you like about these classes? What might you dislike?"
- "So, you're interested in studying business because of the professional opportunities; what business ideas are you interested in? What skills do you think you need to succeed in business?"
- "How great that you love the humanities! Can you articulate why you like them? What skills do you have that make humanities classes especially enjoyable? How could you explore possible paths for graduates with humanities degrees?"
- "I'm sorry to hear how unhappy you have been as a computer science major. What is it about these sorts of classes that you dislike?"

- "Envision yourself academically thriving next semester. What would that look like?"

The sample questions will provoke thinking in students. Without providing space for students to pause and ponder, an academic advisor might jump directly into offering solutions. Self-reflect and learn lays the groundwork for reasoned decision-making. Imagine the following responses from an advisor to the student wary about pursuing a humanities major.

- "How about choosing a different major?"
- "You shouldn't worry about your career now; you're so young."
- "What if you stick with the major for another semester and then decide if you want to switch?"

While none of these responses are necessarily harmful, they decidedly do not prompt student reflection, do not engage or empower critical thinking, and do not spark the development of student agency. As examined in Chapter 2, academic coaching has much in common with appreciative advising with the aim of moving far beyond transactional interactions to helping students explore, discover, and then pursue their academic dreams (Bloom et al., 2008). Consider this description of appreciative advising and note the similarities with academic coaching,

> By using positive open-ended questions designed to uncover students' stories as well as their hopes and dreams for the future, Appreciative Advisors seek to create positive change and help students optimize their educational experiences by partnering with them to co-create a plan for making their hopes and dreams a reality.
>
> (Bloom et al., 2014, p. 7)

CAREER SERVICES

The principles of academic coaching are a good fit for the wealth of programs provided by career services professionals on college campuses. Whether working with a student on career exploration, resume review, job or internship search, or networking and interview skills, there are many natural applications of a coach approach.

Some skills needed to build and transition to life after graduating from college include identifying and articulating a vision of one's future, reflecting on strengths and weaknesses, setting goals, and executing a plan. These are among the many benefits students gain when they participate in conversations infused with a coach approach. Whether a student has a clear picture of their future or not, and regardless of their degree of readiness in entering the workforce or a graduate program, employing academic coaching principles will enhance a career service professional's work with students.

Imagine a college senior whose dream of working for a corporate investment firm has not yet come to fruition; of the dozens of applications they submitted for position postings, they had only two interviews and zero offers. They are worried and discouraged. A career counselor has many coaching tools at their fingertips to navigate a conversation with this student. Consider imagined soundbites from the expanded coaching tools that could be especially helpful.

- Acknowledge: "This must be so frustrating for you because I know how much effort you put into your applications."
- Articulate: "It sounds like you're saying you need to rethink your entire career plan; is that correct?"
- Champion: "You are well prepared for a position in corporate finance, and you have many strengths that an employer will value."
- Intrude: "I want to encourage you to avoid calling yourself a failure because it's factually untrue."
- Reframe: "I know you are concerned you won't ever land your dream job but are there other ways you can look at the current situation?"
- Request/challenge: "I'd like to challenge you to expand your search beyond your target city. I know you'd really like to stay in the Chicago area, but if you're open to the idea, could you investigate positions available elsewhere? What do you think?"

The sample soundbites illustrate several things: they validate the student's feelings, offer encouragement, and move them toward action. These are the very skills we want students to be able to eventually provide for themselves, as they are associated with greater abilities to bounce back from disappointment. For many college-aged students, the transition to adulthood and the world beyond college is exciting but can also be challenging. As they continue down their life path, they will continue to face new trials, as we all do, and learning to tackle them with a measure of resilience will make them less fraught.

Reframing and request/challenge are often helpful coaching tools, especially in the example of our college senior trying to land a position at an investment firm. Imagine other scenarios within the context of career services where reframing and request/challenge might be useful:

- Providing feedback to a student in their practice interview. "I like how you responded to the opening question, but I'd like to request we practice this response again so that you can be even more succinct."

- Reviewing a resume with a student. "Let's see if you can reframe the volunteering section to better highlight the leadership roles you play."
- Reviewing a resume. "I challenge you to rewrite these descriptions to include stronger verbs."
- Career exploration. "I request that you talk to three instructors in the psychology department to get their take on the two graduate programs you are considering."
- Career exploration. "Could you reframe your concern about your set of experiences as it relates to the internship you want?"

These are just a few of the many applications of using the important skills of reframing and request/challenge in a career services context. Career and executive coaching are two of the most prevalent forms of coaching (Yates, 2022), and elements of the academic coaching model can help further adapt these principles and methods to a higher education context.

ACCESSIBILITY SERVICES

Staff in accessibility services departments (sometimes named disability services) interact with students with a wide range of needs and concerns. They also communicate regularly with faculty and staff across their campuses. Whether a member of a campus community has a temporary or permanent disability or medical condition, and whether it is physical or mental, accessibility services is responsible for ensuring that their college experience is accessible. Therefore, staff collaborate with students and faculty to determine accommodations to mitigate barriers associated with a disability. Likewise, accessibility services communicates with faculty and other offices about accommodations and collaborates with them to modify curriculum, websites, and physical spaces to improve accessibility.

Because of the broad reach within their campus communities, staff in accessibility services have many opportunities to utilize a coach approach. Let's consider a few.

While many college students received accommodations or had an Individualized Educational Program (IEP) in high school, many did not. And for those who received accommodations before entering college, higher education is guided by the Americans with Disabilities Act (ADA), which fundamentally changes how accommodations are received. All students, therefore, will need to navigate a new system (Quinn & Maitland, 2011). Beyond providing information about their department's policies and procedures, accessibility services staff can use academic coaching principles to prepare students to navigate the accommodations process effectively. Open-ended questions, such as the examples below, could be instrumental.

- "What might be helpful considerations before you take your test at a different time and location than your classmates?"
- "Since you'll be receiving extra time on your test, what might you need to think about to sustain your energy and focus?"
- "Because you've never used text-to-speech software before, reading in this manner will be different. What do you know about yourself when learning something new? What might you need to make the process smoother?"

Another application of academic coaching is promoting self-advocacy skills, a common topic of interest for accessibility services staff. Academic coaching helps foster self-determination in college students with disabilities (Field et al., 2013; Parker & Boutelle, 2009; Richman et al., 2014). A student who understands their strengths, weaknesses, and how their disability impacts them will have an easier time managing the accommodations process (and, by extension, they will be stronger students overall). The range of disability awareness and acceptance among students is broad, which offers accessibility services staff ample opportunities to meet students wherever they may be. Also, the goal-oriented nature of academic coaching lends itself nicely to helping students learn to identify and articulate their needs around self-advocacy.

For example, students intimidated by the idea of talking to professors about accommodations would benefit from a conversation that encourages them to reflect on their goals and then create an action plan. Sample coaching-infused soundbites might include:

- "What would you like your instructor to know about how you learn best?"
- "In an ideal world, how could your instructor's teaching style make class lectures easier to comprehend?"
- "If you were to imagine a conversation with your instructor that flowed smoothly and where you felt confident, what would it look like?"

One final example of implementing academic coaching with accessibility services staff is how they communicate with faculty. It is not uncommon for faculty to have questions about students' accommodations. Also, certain accommodations requests are more complicated and require ongoing dialogue between the accessibility services office and faculty. Coaching skills could enhance communication, easing the way to an effective solution.

For example, when discussing a complicated accommodation request, accessibility services staff and faculty want to ensure that they don't fundamentally alter the requirements of the course. Let's say a student with diagnosed ADHD and anxiety requested to use a formula sheet on their calculus exams to address their struggle with making errors due to impulsivity. Accessibility staff could reject the request outright based on the student's diagnosis. Or they could ask the faculty to decide whether fulfilling the request would give the student an unfair advantage. The principles of academic coaching could help accessibility services staff lead a collaborative conversation to understand the nature of the class better and arrive at sensible solutions. The sample questions below could generate a fruitful dialogue:

- "How might using a formula sheet on the exam hinder your ability to measure the student's understanding of the material?"
- "If the student continued with further math classes, would they be at a disadvantage if they don't memorize formulas?"
- "What ideas or strategies do you have in helping students memorize tricky formulas?"

The fundamental coaching tool of curiosity is always helpful regardless of the situation. In the scenario above, curiosity could be especially useful in reaching an accommodation decision that is in the student's best interest and that also upholds the integrity of the course.

ADDITIONAL DEPARTMENTS AND PROGRAMS IN STUDENT AFFAIRS

Many departments and programs are housed under the large umbrella of student affairs, with an overarching mission of enhancing the quality of students' lives while they pursue their academic degrees. We've already discussed career services and accessibility services, which are commonly part of student affairs. The scope of departments, programs, and services within student affairs is large and varied enough from college to college to make it impractical to discuss them all in this chapter. However, we will briefly highlight how implementing academic coaching principles could enrich interactions with students in several departments.

Housing and Residential Life

Full-time staff and student employees often make up housing staff, engaging with students on multiple fronts: room assignments, issues with fellow residents, safety, co-curricular programs, and much more. Regardless of the staff's particular role in housing, foundational academic coaching skills can be beneficial. Consider the following examples:

- Assisting students with the adjustment to living away from home for the first time lends itself to the coaching skills of acknowledgment, championing, and request/challenge. "I hear how unsettled you are still feeling living here on campus. I'm also proud of your good progress by joining your suitemates for dinner rather than eating alone in your room. Are you ready for another challenge? How about committing to attending at least one of the social events offered in your residential community this coming weekend?"

- Assisting resident advisors (student staff) to develop programming ideas for first-year students is a good time to lean into the second and third phases of the coaching conversation (self-reflect and learn, explore options and actions). "What do you want your residents to gain from the program? How will you know if it's successful? What ideas do you have to engage the students? What are some potential pitfalls?"

Student Wellness

Student wellness programs vary from institution to institution. However, the general mission among them is to provide services and programs that contribute to students' well-being on several dimensions, including but not limited to physical, emotional, and social. Students can get support around drug and alcohol use, financial management, stress management, healthy relationships, nutritious eating, and much more. Universities are also implementing wellness coaching programs to support student health and well-being (Gibbs & Larcus, 2015). The examples below are just a fraction of the many applications of academic coaching within the context of student wellness:

- Staff working with students around making healthy food choices can encourage them to reflect on their overall health goals and identify reasonable steps they can take to make progress on these goals. "What one or two small meal-prep changes can you make in the week ahead to reflect your goal of wanting more energy? What are a few new vegetables you could add to your meals this week to expand your diet?"
- Like the above, staff can help students reflect on their lifestyle goals when creating a monthly budget. "How could your spending choices each month reflect your values? If you wanted to have more money set aside for socializing with friends—one of your goals—how could you shift your spending elsewhere? Since you want to know where your money goes each month, what ideas do you have to better track your spending?"

Student Conduct

Student conduct departments support their institution's mission of maintaining a safe and accountable environment. Staff work with students to ensure they understand school policies, guide them in making responsible choices that align with these policies, and, when necessary, hold them to account when they breach standards. Student conduct departments often oversee an honor court where students are employed to review misconduct claims. Reflect on how incorporating academic coaching skills, exemplified in the soundbites below, aids student growth.

- Staff helping a student better understand the consequences of their actions. "Bring yourself back to the night of the party. What might have been a critical choice that ultimately led you to this hazing infraction? Before attending future parties, what steps can you take to ensure you make good choices? Imagine talking to an older and wiser version of yourself; what advice might they offer?"
- Permanent staff encouraging student staff to set boundaries with friends who ask for inside information about honor court proceedings. "I want to affirm that you are in a tricky situation when friends want you to share private information you have access to as a member of the honor court. What is difficult about setting boundaries with friends on this front? What if we brainstormed a few responses you might have at the ready for any future inquiries you may get from friends?"

WRAPPING UP

The goal of this chapter is not a call to upend the ways you work with students and start anew with the principles of academic coaching. Rather, the goal is to illustrate that regardless of one's role in their department and on their campus, or if they interact with students even briefly, staff can apply elements of the academic coaching model. This is true regardless of the length and type of interaction. By finding opportunities to give students space to reflect, problem-solve, and plan, students will benefit. Professionals such as counselors, teachers, and coaches know that the fruit of their work might bloom long after they have left the picture. It is not uncommon for an academic coach to believe they held a less than inspiring coaching session, only to be surprised when the student returns for more coaching. Despite appearances and interpretations to the contrary during an initial conversation, they wanted another coaching conversation. Astonishingly enough for the coach, an idea for the student sunk in or sparked interest.

We all would do well to never underestimate how our conversations and interactions impact others, especially those with college students. And this is precisely why when staff find ways to implement elements of coaching into their work with students, even through small and subtle changes, they will have played a part in laying the seeds for change in the student.

Next, we look at considerations in applying the academic coaching model when working with a great diversity of college students.

REFERENCES

Bloom, J. L., Hutson, B. L., & He, Y. (2008). *The appreciative advising revolution*. Stipes Publishing.

Bloom, J. L., Hutson, B. L., He, Y., & Konkle, E. (2014). *The appreciative advising revolution training workbook: Translating theory to practice*. Stipes Publishing L.L.C.

Clemons, C., Rademacher, K., & Howlett, M. A. (2018, October 11). *Coaching and tutoring: The benefits of a shared approach to academic support*. Annual Conference of the College Reading and Learning Association, Albuquerque, NM.

Field, S., Parker, D. R., Sawilowsky, S., & Rolands, L. (2013). Assessing the impact of ADHD coaching services on university students' learning skills, self-regulation, and well-being. *Journal of Postsecondary Education and Disability, 26*(1), 67–81. https://files.eric.ed.gov/fulltext/EJ1026813.pdf

Gibbs, T., & Larcus, J. (2015). Wellness coaching: Helping students thrive. *Journal of Student Affairs, 24*(23), 23–34.

Kimsey-House, H., Kimsey-House, K., Sandahl, P., & Whitworth, L. (2018). *Co-Active Coaching: The proven framework for transformative conversations at work and life* (4th ed.). Nicholas Brealey Publishing.

Lipsky, S. A. (2011). *A training guide for college tutors and peer educators*. Pearson.

Parker, D. R., & Boutelle, K. (2009). Executive function coaching for college students with learning disabilities and ADHD: A new approach for fostering self-determination. *Learning Disabilities Research & Practice, 24*(4), 204–215. https://doi.org/10.1111/j.1540-5826.2009.00294.x

Quinn, P. O., & Maitland, T. L. (2011). *On your own: A college readiness guide for teens with ADHD/LD*. Magination Press.

Richman, E. L., Rademacher, K. N., & Maitland, T. L. (2014). Coaching and college success. *Journal of Postsecondary Education and Disability, 27*(1), 33–50. https://files.eric.ed.gov/fulltext/EJ1029647.pdf

Saenz, M., Lewis, A., Trumble, S., & Schotka, R. (2021, July). *CRLA international peer educator training program certification standards, outcomes and assessments: Guidance for peer educator training programs level 1* (1st ed.). College Reading and Learning Association. https://www.crla.net/images/IPTPC/CRLA-IPTPC-SOAs-Final-August-16-2021-updates-TOC-September-19-2021.pdf

Toms, M. (2010). *Put the pencil down: Essentials of tutoring*. NC State University Undergraduate Tutorial Center.

Yates, J. (2022). *The career coaching handbook* (2nd ed.). Routledge.

Chapter 12

The Great Diversity of College Students

As discussed in Chapter 2, one primary entry point for coaching in higher education emerged from efforts to support students with ADHD, learning differences, and other forms of disability. Practical experience and empirical research reinforced the effectiveness of coaching for this population of students. Academic coaching in higher education broadened and is now much more commonly available to a wide cross-section of college students. While we believe academic coaching can be helpful to most students, applications and approaches should be considered when working across a range of student populations. In parallel to the beginnings of our work in academic coaching, we'll start this chapter with a discussion of academic coaching with students with ADHD and/or learning differences and expand from there.

You'll note many overlaps between the groups covered in this chapter. The students we meet with may have a range of intersectional identities and backgrounds. The populations discussed here are non-exhaustive, and an entire tome could be dedicated to applications and considerations in providing academic coaching for different student contexts. Lastly, and perhaps most importantly, although we examine academic coaching with a range of student populations in this chapter, we acknowledge that overgeneralizing about college students can be counterproductive, and we reaffirm that each person remains at the heart of academic coaching.

STUDENTS WITH ADHD AND/OR LEARNING DIFFERENCES

As discussed throughout this book, academic coaching can be useful for many students and for many reasons. Students with ADHD, however, are often particularly well suited for academic coaching because of its orientation toward taking action and staying accountable. As a student once said, "I know what I should be doing, but I just don't do it."

DOI: 10.4324/9781003291879-15

While each student with ADHD will have unique experiences, the above sentiment about difficulty taking action can be a common frustration. One reason is that ADHD symptoms frequently impact the brain's executive functioning—the set of cognitive processes and mental skills responsible for attention, working memory, task initiation, planning, organizing, emotional control, and impulse control. There is a substantial overlap between ADHD and executive function deficits (Brown, 2013). However, ADHD is considered a neurodevelopmental disorder whose impact can extend beyond executive functioning skills by posing significant impairments to certain aspects of one's life (Heller & Cooper-Kahn, 2022). These impairments include maintaining interpersonal relationships, managing finances, and meeting expectations of a job or academics.

An ADHD diagnosis can fall into three categories: hyperactive, inattentive, or combined. Features of the hyperactive type include feeling restless and fidgety, excessive talking, and a tendency to blurt or interrupt. Features of the inattentive type include difficulty sustaining attention and effort, easily distracted and forgetful, and a tendency to make careless errors. Of course, the combined type of ADHD will include features from both the hyperactive and inattentive types (CHADD, 2017).

When considering the characteristics of an ADHD diagnosis along with its effect on executive functions, it's easy to understand how some college students might face challenges.

Let's look at the ADHD student's lament about knowing what to do but not doing it.

Imagine this student, whom we'll name Brian, has hyperactive and inattentive ADHD and is in the library trying to study for an economics test scheduled at the end of the week. Though he's set himself up in the library for the sole purpose of reviewing economics, what might get in the way of a productive study session? He might open the textbook and feel overwhelmed by the complexity of the problems and decide to start with a less taxing, low-priority task in a different class. Even though he's cleared his plate to focus only on reviewing economics, he remembered an important email he must respond to and starts drafting a lengthy reply. Digging into time-consuming, challenging concepts seems even more demanding when sitting at his desk for a significant length of time; he frequently gets up and walks around the carrels. Searching his backpack, he realizes he forgot to bring a folder with necessary study handouts from the instructor. He gets distracted by the sights and sounds of other students sitting nearby. He is distracted by the knowledge that his phone, though silenced, is in his backpack—what alerts might he be missing?—so he reaches for his phone and checks. And checks again and again. A friend wanders past him, stops to say hello, and they start talking. And they continue talking while Brian is unaware of time passing. He finally leaves the library and heads home, disappointed in himself for barely scratching the surface of his economics studying.

The above vignette is a classic and highly frustrating experience for a student like Brian with ADHD. Yes, he knew what he should do and what he wanted to do, but he just could not execute his plan.

In a college setting, students are responsible for independently managing nearly every aspect of their lives: time, studies, priorities, materials, and more. Students who intuitively know how to create systems and structures may find managing the multitude of these demands less daunting. For students with ADHD, building systems and structures for themselves may not be intuitive. Again, every student, whether they have ADHD or not, is uniquely influenced by their personal histories, temperaments, strengths, weaknesses, goals, and interests. While students with ADHD will likely share some traits, that doesn't necessarily mean they face identical trials. However, when students lack systems to execute plans, like Brian, they will likely benefit from learning how to build and rely on external structures to keep themselves organized and on-task. Academic coaching can provide the tools for students in this regard. When we take a moment to recall the goals of academic coaching (using open-ended questions so that students can better understand themselves, learn to set and stay accountable to goals, and improve their self-regulation and study strategies), we see how it aligns beautifully with the needs of many students with ADHD (Field et al., 2013; Kennedy, 2017; Parker et al., 2011; Parker & Boutelle, 2009; Richman et al., 2014).

Let's return to Brian and consider how a coach could work with him to address some of his ADHD-related struggles with studying. As a coach would do with any student, a starting point would be to engage Brian with reflective, open-ended questions.

- "Let's come up with a few strategies to try when tackling multi-step, complex economics problems. What ideas do you have to reduce the 'overwhelm' feeling you experience when starting a new problem? If there's another area in your life where you get overwhelmed, how do you currently manage it?"
- "What measures could you put in place to better manage your task list so that you have fewer incidences of remembering things at the last minute— like the email you needed to write during the time you'd reserved for studying."
- "Likewise, what measure could you put in place to ensure your backpack has everything you need before you leave your room?"

Based on how Brian responds to points two and three above, the coach might suggest a few strategies. For example, Brian might consider designating a recurring time each day to review and update his task list. He might use a phone alert to remind him of this routine. He might create a written checklist to refer to when loading his backpack.

Here are more coaching questions for Brian:

- "Should we think about how to take effective breaks when you're feeling antsy and need to move a bit? What kind of break would refuel you and allow you to return to studying? And if sitting for too long is hard, what options might you have to study with minimal sitting?"
- "You were distracted by the sights and sounds of other students in the library; what might you do differently next time you set yourself up to study? What can you do to minimize distractions?"
- "You were also distracted by your phone, even though it was silenced and in your backpack. How can you manage your phone differently going forward?"

As with the first set of questions, the coach could make suggestions based on Brian's responses. For example, Brian might explore studying in different locations on campus to find the environment that gives him optimal attention. He might also experiment with exercising before he studies to see if that helps reduce his feelings of physical restlessness. Or he could try studying at a standing desk. Finally, Brian could experiment with apps that limit or monitor his phone usage.

Recurring academic coaching sessions can be especially beneficial for students like Brian. They could help Brian build momentum and feel accountable and motivated to practice implementing ideas that could serve to add structure to his daily life. Generally, the more structure for Brian, the more he will learn to manage all aspects of his life.

For academic coaches working with students who have ADHD, it is helpful to consider how to enhance the meeting for students. A straightforward discussion with the student about what they need to ensure optimal attention within the academic coaching conversation is a great way to give the student agency. For example, some students need to know it's okay to ask to have something repeated if their attention momentarily drifts away. Some students will focus better with minimal auditory and visual distractions in the meeting space. And when it comes time to the last phase of the coaching conversation—design and commit to plans—taking time to flesh out the finer details is often helpful. For example, questions such as the following might prompt students to think about adding even more structure to their plan:

- "How will you remember this plan so you'll know your next steps even after you leave here and go about your day?"
- "I see you've taken notes about what you'd like to try differently next week; where will these notes live so that you can refer to them?"
- "If you want to make sure you're getting ready for bed by 11:00 pm to ensure more rest, what do you need to help make this happen? What

exactly do you want to do, and how long will you need to get ready for bed? Will you know when it's 11:00 pm to begin getting ready, or will you need an alert?"

Academic coaching is not only effective for students who have ADHD, but it's also effective for students with other learning differences. Many learning differences impact reading, writing, math, and information processing—too many to go into detail here. The piece to understand is that the spirit of academic coaching, which helps students better understand themselves to devise and implement strategies accordingly, can be tremendously beneficial for those navigating learning differences.

We'll look at one brief example. Imagine a student, Keisha, who has a diagnosed reading disorder. She struggles to find time to read the volume of pages assigned to her weekly in each class because her speed is slow. She can also miss key takeaways. Through conversations with her academic coach, Keisha experiments with text readers that provide auditory versions of printed text. Keisha also tests out reading in smaller chunks and at different times of the day to see if dispersing the reading helps with her fatigue. Keisha and her coach discuss sharing her concerns with instructors and requesting suggestions on where to focus her time and attention when reading the assignments.

The academic coaching process helps students like Keisha articulate the impact of her learning difference, which is an essential starting point in collaborating with a coach to explore accommodations, study strategies, and potential workarounds.

UNDERREPRESENTED STUDENTS

We believe that academic coaching provides an effective framework for working with students with a wide variety of backgrounds and identities. The approach is student-centered and individualized. Academic coaching also occurs within broader societal systems and structures that include discrimination, racism, sexism, homophobia, and more. In this section, we examine in greater detail how academic coaching can be used in working with a wide range of students, particularly with students from historically underrepresented and marginalized groups.

We'll begin with some of the strengths of the academic coaching model in working with underrepresented students. One of the most pertinent components here is that we clearly affirm that a student knows much more about themselves than their coach. A coach has tremendous expertise. But in terms of a student's lived experience, strengths, weaknesses, situation, hopes, dreams, challenges, and more the student is the expert on their life. A primary goal of academic coaching is developing an empowering, collaborative relationship in contrast to one that may be disempowering and invalidating.

For students, no matter their identities or background, as coaches we don't know exactly what their life is like for them. Sure, there are times when we can relate to things they say or experiences they have, but it's not the case that we can say "we've been there." This is especially true for coaches with majority or privileged identities when working with students with non-majority identities. That doesn't mean we can't affirm, empathize, or normalize when working with students. When appropriate, a coach saying something like, "I've heard many students describe similar experiences" can be powerful for a student to hear. And we can always thank students for sharing their experiences and ideas with us. Listening is a foundation of academic coaching, and really listening to students can help counter the biases and prejudices that undergird systemic racism and discrimination (McGuire, 2020).

Academic support services can be an impactful context for microaffirmations in higher education (Powell et al., 2013). Microaffirmations can be defined as acts that advance inclusion, affirmation, listening, and support (Rowe, 2008). One cornerstone of academic coaching is the direct interpersonal work of being there with the student. "I see you." "I hear you." "I appreciate you." "I'm so glad to meet with you today." While these statements may seem basic, they can be incredibly affirming. In academic coaching appointments, we can tell students, "You belong here." Channeling the expanded skill of articulation, coaches underscore, "I see your hard work and efforts." Microaffirmations can help foster a more inclusive environment for academic coaching.

If we want to improve the effectiveness of our work in supporting a broad diversity of students, it is often most impactful to start with ourselves. Resources on advancing diversity, equity, and inclusion in higher education frequently recommend examining one's own personal biases (Addy et al., 2021; Carnes et al., 2012; Cuyjet et al., 2016; Puckett & Lind, 2020). And in developing greater cultural competence, it's both imperative and challenging to become more aware of our own cultural and societal conditioning (Adler & Gundersen, 2008). Before we can better account for and counteract our own personal biases, we must recognize them. Circling back to the academic coaching definition in Chapter 3, one core element is to help students "understand their habits and thinking patterns." All of the principles and fundamental beliefs in academic coaching apply equally to coaches. As coaches, we all have thinking patterns that lead us to making assumptions or prematurely inferring things about people and situations, and when we're working with students from marginalized groups these biases and assumptions can be particularly deleterious.

If one of the launching points is starting with ourselves, it is also critical to expand our listening to learn about the experiences of others, especially those from underrepresented and marginalized groups. Learning more about topics like systemic racism and structural inequalities, though possibly uncomfortable, is an important aspect of becoming more effective coaches and higher education professionals (Aguilar, 2020; Baron & Azizollah, 2018; Hale, Jr., 2004; McGuire, 2020). Differences in identities, backgrounds, experiences, and contexts make the fundamental tool of managing self even more important. We typically aim to limit the provision of direct advice to students for many reasons, and one of them is because of potential differences in contexts and backgrounds. Advice such as "You should quit your job to focus on classes," may be insensitive or demeaning.

Much of this work returns to the concept of a person-centered form of academic support. In working with students who may have different backgrounds and identities than our own, we approach the conversations with curiosity and openness and do our best to resist assumptions. We approach working with students from a place of strength, *their* strength. We don't pander or paternalize. Even well-meaning coaches wanting to create inclusive spaces can occasionally slide into a conversation with microaggressions. Sue et al. define racial microaggressions as "brief and commonplace daily verbal, behavioral, and environmental indignities, whether intentional or unintentional, that communicate hostile, derogatory, or negative racial slights and insults to the target person or group" (2007, p. 273).

Scholarship from the world of academic advising, which shares many similarities with academic coaching, helps illustrate how higher education programs and services can positively impact the success of students from diverse student populations. Museus recommends that white advisors can bolster their effectiveness of working

> with students of color by investing energy in understanding the struggles these students face, committing to continuously learning about these experiences, and reflexively working to understand their own privilege and how they can use it to empower students from marginalized communities and help them thrive.
>
> (2021, p. 28)

A similar approach can be taken to improve an academic coach's work with LGBTQ students, students who are differently abled, and more. Academic coaching is all about growth and development over time. These principles apply to academic coaches just as much if not more so than the students with whom we work.

FIRST-GENERATION COLLEGE STUDENTS

Many of the considerations and approaches from the previous section on academic coaching with students from underrepresented and marginalized groups apply to work with first-generation college students (first-gen students). And there can be extensive overlap between all these populations. As enrollment at institutions of higher education continues to diversify, many students will become the first in their families to graduate from college. First-gen students can face a variety of obstacles, including differing levels of academic preparation, access to social capital, and less access to resources such as financial supports (Pratt et al., 2019; Saenz et al., 2007). While many first-gen students have supportive families, there can be less immediate familial knowledge of the complexities and contours of higher education. Colleges have unique language, processes, structures, traditions, and more that can be opaque to those without insider knowledge. First-gen students may find academic coaching particularly beneficial to aid in acclimating to their new environment. At least one study has found that first-gen students were more likely to use voluntary academic coaching than students who had at least one parent graduate from college (Grabsch et al., 2021).

One key to providing academic coaching to this group of students is to resist assumptions and stereotypes. In some institutions, unless a student voluntarily self-discloses that they are a first-gen student, staff would not know their familial educational history. Without access to a student's background, it is likely easier to resist assumptions. Regardless of what we do and do not know about our students, it's important to counter potential typecasts about their educational background based on race, ethnicity, place of birth, and more. Once more, the foundational academic coaching tools of managing self and being curious are critical to working with students. When academic coaches meet with students, we channel our curiosity to ask them open-ended questions that promote reflection which can serve to short-circuit the possible slide into making assumptions.

As academic coaches, it's also important to remember that the students we meet with have varying levels of academic preparation as well as fluency in the inner workings of higher education. We aim to avoid jargon and unexplained terminology. One common suggestion in academic support is to "go to office hours." That can be easier said than done. And we must remember that some students might not know what office hours are, or why going might be helpful, or what to do once they get there, or that the situation might be intimidating (Hogan & Sathy, 2022, pp. 163–164). "I don't even know what to ask or say," is a common statement from students. The third phase of the coaching conversation, explore options and actions, can be fruitful in this instance, and the student could role-play their visit to office hours with an academic coach.

Academic coaches can serve an important role as guides and interpreters for students navigating college. Some students may not be familiar with the norms and conventions of higher education in the United States, which can be particularly challenging for first-gen students and international students (see the upcoming section in this chapter). Some students might be faced with writing a paper for the first time in which they make their own argument in conversation with other scholars in the field. They might not have an idea of how to make an original argument, and they might be intimidated by the prospect of disagreeing with their professor. As guides we can connect students to resources like a writing center or a book like *They Say, I Say* (Graff & Birkenstein, 2021), and we can work directly with students to unpack these conventions. We can ask open-ended questions like, "Why does your professor want to hear what you think about this topic?" or "How might making an argument demonstrate what you've learned about the material?"

The academic coaching model is helpful in working with students who are grappling with elements related to imposter syndrome. Feeling like you don't belong or that you shouldn't be in college can occur within a broad range of students, and it can be especially prominent for students who are the first in their family to go to college. Students may have had varying levels of preparation or access to opportunities, and some are balancing extensive work and familial responsibilities in addition to their college academics. We ask students who might feel that they don't belong, "What gifts do you bring?" and "What are your strengths?" Using the expanded skills from Chapter 7 such as reframing and championing can help students identify their strengths and their reasons for belonging. A coach can share,

I've seen how much effort you've put into your term paper while putting in additional time helping out with your family. You may not have received the grade you were wanting, but another perspective is that during an immensely challenging semester you began and completed the longest paper you ever wrote and learned a lot about researching in the process.

College staff and faculty can play a significant role in validating and valuing the lived experiences of first-gen students (Ellis et al., 2019).

TRANSFER STUDENTS

Students transfer from one institution to another for a myriad of reasons. Some move from a community college to a four-year college as part of an intentional plan to earn a four-year degree at a lower cost or by easing into a more demanding experience. Some transfer from one four-year school to another due to financial or academic hardship. Students might transfer after deciding to major in a program not available at their original school or because they seek a different social environment. Non-traditionally aged students might enroll at an institution as transfer students to finish earning their undergraduate degree which they'd started years earlier. Of the non-traditional transfer students, some might be veterans, some could simultaneously be working and raising families, and some could be first-generation college students.

With the variety of life experiences transfer students have and the type of motivators driving them to enroll as transfers, many needs and challenges for

139

these students emerge. For example, they can feel like a first-year student again even though they have attended college elsewhere—they must acclimate anew to a different campus community which takes time, energy, and resilience. Transfer students can be frustrated to discover that not all credits earned at their original institution count toward their major requirement at their new school, which may in turn affect time-to-degree-completion requirements (Jenkins & Fink, 2015). When students transfer to a more academically rigorous school, their level of preparedness might be inadequate. Similarly, non-traditional students, despite having a wealth of adult experiences, might find that their academic skills are rusty or do not easily translate to an academic world that has been transformed since last they attended college. Feeling socially isolated is another common struggle for transfer students; forming friendships as the "new kid" or "older person" is not always easy.

In addition to dedicated programs colleges might have to support transfer students, staff and faculty can enhance the experience for students by using academic coaching skills. As discussed throughout the book and particularly in this chapter, a strength of academic coaching is that it empowers students to articulate their needs and goals in an individualized, holistic manner. The ground for progress and growth is fertile when students—including transfers—have the space and encouragement to reflect on their needs, explore resources and strategies, and ultimately act on plans. Academic support programs and other campus resources may be particularly important to transfer students navigating the transition to a new college (Daddona et al., 2021; Ellis, 2013; Flaga, 2006; Walker & Okpala, 2017).

Like all students, transfer students want to feel welcomed, included, and valued at their institution. By being aware of and sensitive to the distinct and diverse circumstances transfers bring to the table, staff and faculty can assist these students as they adjust and acclimate. The following open-ended coaching questions would help lay that very groundwork:

- "What academic skills do you already have, and what skills do you think you need to succeed (either in general or in particular classes)?"
- "Based on your background and the experiences you've accrued in your life thus far, what unique contributions can you make in class? To the campus community?"
- "What most excites you about this campus (classes, instructors, residence hall, peers, etc.)? What surprises you, either positively or negatively?"
- "What opportunities would you like to take advantage of here?"
- "Because you are at a much larger school, what might you do to create smaller communities for yourself?"
- "How might you rethink your graduation timeline given the degree requirements for your major?"

When talking with a transfer student who might be discouraged and disappointed with their academic performance or who may be generally overwhelmed by the adjustment, the coaching skills of acknowledgment and reframing would be beneficial. It is incredibly validating to have someone acknowledge the challenge during a difficult time. "Yes, transferring is no small thing." "Many students struggle with this class." "Returning to college after a ten-year hiatus must be very disorienting."

Equally valuable is having someone help to reframe the situation. "Rather than viewing these past two weeks as failures, how about viewing them as evidence that you are still adjusting?" "I know how frustrated you are that one of your biology credits did not transfer, but I wonder if retaking that class at this school might ultimately benefit you? Can you think of any upsides?"

Transfer students can make many valuable contributions that will enrich their academic communities; coaching conversations can be one factor in creating pathways for their contributions.

INTERNATIONAL STUDENTS

In the continuing diversification of higher education, one of the more rapidly growing populations is that of international students. As with all of the groups in this chapter, one must be cautious in generalizations about international students as these are students coming to college from all corners of the globe and students who hail from the same country or city may arrive with vastly different educational backgrounds. Even within the same university, the academic support needs for undergraduate international students may be distinct from their graduate student counterparts. As a note, we write this chapter from the perspective of academic coaches working at a higher education institution in the United States.

One recurring theme from this chapter is that we maintain that the overarching academic coaching model can be successfully implemented with a broad range of students in large part because of the individualized, student-centered nature of academic coaching. We take the same overall approach to work with international students while continually collaborating with the student in an effort to make the service as effective as possible. Some international students may be new to the United States while others may have many years of lived experience within the country. We believe everyone brings with them strengths. Going to college is an achievement for everyone, and university study in a country different from where you grew up is even more impressive. That said, as with other students, we don't want to pander to or paternalize students we work with.

American universities have norms, expectations, processes, and structures that may be different from the educational systems in the home countries of international students (He et al., 2016). Academic coaching, which strives to be collaborative and non-hierarchical, might not map onto the experiences of some students. Here again, it's important to not simply assume that everyone will immediately understand and be comfortable with this interpersonal model of academic support, and there may be instances where modifications or additional clarification may be needed. Academic coaches can explain that they purposefully use this collaborative approach and this experience will be useful for the international student in becoming more comfortable and confident in navigating American higher education. As academic coaches we pay attention to a student's engagement and overall comfort, checking in regularly to see what would be helpful to them, and refining our approach to better support the student. Coaches can also serve as important guides and cultural informants, helping international students better understand and navigate the norms and conventions of American higher education (Taylor, 2007).

STEM STUDENTS

While academic coaching in working with STEM students is largely similar to non-STEM students, additional considerations and approaches may be pertinent. As discussed throughout this book, in academic coaching we try to minimize giving advice or solving students' problems for them. One reason for this is that for topics students bring to academic coaching, there tends to not be correct answers. When working with students in STEM or other related fields, there might very well be a correct answer to a student's question. It's still critical to remember that the student retains control and agency during the conversation. Academic coaching is not office hours, a review session, or a tutoring session (though utilizing aspects of academic coaching in these contexts was discussed in greater detail in Chapter 10).

In working with STEM students, self-management can become even more important, especially if students are interested in working on topics related to content. When STEM students come to academic coaching, our focus is helping them understand how and why a problem is correct. Put another way, it's one thing to get the answer right, and it's another to understand why. Many students might approach STEM homework from a "correct answer" perspective. Some online modules provide students an unlimited number of attempts to select the correct answer, allowing a person to continue guessing the solution without deepening their understanding of the material. Some students may rely on the help of friends or family members for answers. At other times, students can mechanically get the right answer but without thinking critically or flexibly. In short, doing well on homework does not necessarily mean a student understands the material at higher orders of thinking.

Academic coaching can support students in using more active and engaged approaches to STEM learning. Strategies and approaches pertaining to metacognition and self-regulated learning may be particularly important to students in STEM classes (Arslantas et al., 2018; National Research Council, 2012). An academic coach can encourage students to show their work including the steps within the problem and their thought processes. They can also ask students to walk them through and narrate problems. Coaches ask open-ended questions to further and deepen learning, such as: "How does this work? What concepts does this problem draw on? What's similar and different here from what you've learned elsewhere in the course?"

Academic coaching can also help shift a student's perspective on homework and assignments. This might take some convincing, understandably, since many students have been conditioned from an early age to view homework as a chore to complete before doing things that are fun. Children are often told: "You must do your homework before you can play with your friends." They aren't typically told that homework is an important tool for furthering, deepening, and solidifying their learning. And, let's be frank, some assignments are more conducive to developing students' higher-order learning and thinking than others. Viewing homework as a chore to be completed quickly, of course, is not limited to STEM students. In working with a wide range of students, we can ask, "What's the purpose of your professor having you do this assignment?" "What do they want you to get out of it?" "What do they want you to learn from this assignment?" "Professors can assign all varieties of problems or reading or activities, why did they ask you to do this?" Thinking through and answering these types of questions help students become more active participants in their coursework, which will directly support their learning.

GRADUATE STUDENTS

While much of this book is dedicated to academic coaching for undergraduate students, the model is applicable and effective to working with graduate students. Academic support programs for graduate students have been relatively rare, although more recently there have been concerted efforts to provide programs to graduate students similar to what have been more traditionally available to undergraduates (Hardré & Hackett, 2015; Sheehy, 2016). Perhaps it's understandable, at least on surface levels, why academic support for graduate students has generally been overlooked. After all, graduate students, by definition, are some of the most successful students out there. For someone becoming a dentist, getting a master's degree, or writing a dissertation, why would they need additional support?

We frequently say that one of the gifts of academic coaching is that many of the topics, strategies, and approaches in this work with college students are applicable well past graduation. As life proceeds, there are still projects to begin, work on, and complete. We manage multiple priorities. We create and follow systems to organize our time. We battle against procrastination and push through periods of low motivation. We seek out opportunities for growth and development. We work by ourselves, in pairs, and in teams. The challenges and the opportunities for growth continue, and within an academic context, perhaps these challenges are amplified with graduate students.

Academic coaching is well suited for providing academic support to graduate students. As a personal example, Marc utilized academic coaching extensively while completing his PhD at UNC-Chapel Hill. Kristen was one of his coaches! Let's use Marc's history with academic coaching as a window into the applications of this model with graduate students. Marc excelled academically growing up, in college, and during his master's program. He took school seriously, perhaps too seriously. In college, he received only one B, and he's still angry at Professor Beck for giving him a B+ in the Sociology of the Arts!

However, over the course of a PhD program at UNC-Chapel Hill things began faltering. Marc struggled with some coursework, earning the lowest grades in his cohort on a variety of papers and projects. His confidence began to decline. The academic enterprise became much more challenging when reaching the dissertation stage of the PhD program. The years stretched out. Marc, begrudgingly, continued to update the "Expected graduation date" section of his CV. In meetings with his advisor and over email, Marc promised to get things done. Weeks went by and little progress was made. Marc had become a student who rarely followed through on his academic plans and promises.

Fortunately, in the midst of dissertation floundering, Marc joined the Learning Center as a graduate student providing academic coaching. Immediately, he saw the utility of a service that could complement the efforts of his advisor and committee. And since the academic coaches weren't the ones with the authority to sign off on his PhD work, Marc felt more comfortable being vulnerable and real about ongoing struggles. Working with academic coaches, he not just developed plans but enacted them.

One watershed moment during an academic coaching appointment occurred in the design and commit to plans phase when Marc committed to emailing every member of his committee to set up a one-on-one meeting. He hadn't communicated with some of these professors in over a year. That one, seemingly simple action accelerated progress to completion. To help elevate his flagging motivation, Marc and his coaches collaboratively brainstormed different ideas and came up with the idea of tracking his dissertation hours on spreadsheets and then making graphs out of them. Yes, that sounds a bit weird, but for Marc seeing charts of average dissertation hours worked inspired even more productivity.

The structure and accountability of academic coaching was key, especially in collaborating on the role of accountability. People in Marc's life were kind, and almost everyone seemed to let him off the hook for things. Knowing this, Marc asked his academic coaches to hold him to account and ask pointed questions like, "You said this was your goal for the past week. What happened? Is the goal no longer important to you?" All of that helped tremendously, and after eight years he finally finished his PhD and graduated (Howlett, 2015).

WRAPPING UP

Academic coaching is a powerful, individualized method for providing academic support to college students. The fundamental beliefs discussed in detail in Chapter 4 constitute the foundation for this student-centered practice, recognizing and valuing that everyone we work with is a unique person. However, we must not forget that there may be other factors affecting our interpersonal work. Today's universities and college students are incredibly diverse places. Such great diversity is to be celebrated. At universities, there's increased emphasis on championing diversity, actively countering racism, expanding services to support students from marginalized groups, and reckoning with institutional history. Academic coaching occurs within all these overarching systems, structures, and contexts. And there's still much work to be done.

For the individual academic coach, perhaps it is most important for us to work on identifying, acknowledging, and then countering our own personal biases. We all bring a multitude of perspectives and beliefs to an academic coaching conversation, and we continually endeavor to resist making assumptions, overgeneralizing, or succumbing to stereotypes.

While academic coaching is interpersonal work, often within a one-on-one context, we also must remember that every student navigates a world with much larger systems and structures. Each coach's experience within these systems and structures is different, sometimes very different, from the students with whom we work. As such, humility paired with curiosity is vital to the human-centered work of being an academic coach.

REFERENCES

Addy, T. M., Dube, D., Mitchell, K. A., & SoRelle, M. E. (2021). *What inclusive instructors do: Principles and practices for excellence in college teaching.* Stylus Publishing.

Adler, N. J., & Gundersen, A. (2008). *International dimensions of organizational behavior* (5th ed.). Thomson South-Western.

Aguilar, E. (2020). *Coaching for equity: Conversations that change practice.* Jossey-Bass.

Arslantas, F., Wood, E., & MacNeil, S. (2018). Metacognitive foundations in higher education chemistry. In C. Cox & W. Schatzberg (Eds.), *International perspectives on chemistry education research and practice* (pp. 57–77). American Chemical Society.

Baron, H., & Azizollah, H. (2018). Coaching and diversity. In S. Palmer & A. Whybrow (Eds.), *Handbook of coaching psychology: A guide for practitioners* (2nd ed., pp. 500–511). Routledge.

Brown, T. E. (2013). *A new understanding of ADHD in children and adults: Executive function impairments*. Routledge.

Carnes, M., Devine, P. G., Isaac, C., Manwell, L. B., Ford, C. E., Byars-Winston, A., Fine, E., & Sheridan, J. (2012). Promoting institutional change through bias literacy. *Journal of Diversity in Higher Education, 5*(2), 63. https://doi.org/10.1037/a0028128

CHADD. (2017). *Diagnosis of ADHD in adults*. https://chadd.org/for-adults/diagnosis-of-adhd-in-adults/

Cuyjet, M. J., Linder, C., Howard-Hamilton, M. F., & Cooper, D. L. (Eds.). (2016). *Multiculturalism on campus: Theory, models, and practices for understanding diversity and creating inclusion* (2nd ed.). Stylus Publishing.

Daddona, M. F., Mondie-Milner, C., & Goodson, J. (2021). Transfer student resources: Keeping students once they enroll. *Journal of College Student Retention: Research, Theory & Practice, 23*(3), 487–506. https://doi.org/10.1177/1521025119848754

Ellis, J. M., Powell, C. S., Demetriou, C. P., Huerta-Bapat, C., & Panter, A. T. (2019). Examining first-generation college student lived experiences with microaggressions and microaffirmations at a predominately White public research university. *Cultural Diversity and Ethnic Minority Psychology, 25*(2), 266. https://doi.org/10.1037/cdp0000198

Ellis, M. M. (2013). Successful community college transfer students speak out. *Community College Journal of Research and Practice, 37*(2), 73–84. https://doi.org/10.1080/10668920903304914

Field, S., Parker, D. R., Sawilowsky, S., & Rolands, L. (2013). Assessing the impact of ADHD coaching services on university students' learning skills, self-regulation, and well-being. *Journal of Postsecondary Education and Disability, 26*(1), 67–81. https://files.eric.ed.gov/fulltext/EJ1026813.pdf

Flaga, C. T. (2006). The process of transition for community college transfer students. *Community College Journal of Research and Practice, 30*(1), 3–19. https://doi.org/10.1080/10668920500248845

Grabsch, D. K., Peña, R. A., & Parks, K. J. (2021). Expectations of students participating in voluntary peer academic coaching. *Journal of College Reading and Learning, 51*(2), 95–109. https://doi.org/10.1080/10790195.2020.1798827

Graff, G., & Birkenstein, C. (2021). *They say/I say* (5th ed.). W.W. Norton & Company.

Hale, Jr., F. W. (Ed.). (2004). *What makes racial diversity work in higher education: Academic leaders present successful policies and strategies*. Stylus Publishing.

Hardré, P. L., & Hackett, S. M. (2015). Understanding the graduate college experience: Perceptual differences by degree type, point-in-program and disciplinary subgroups. *Learning Environments Research, 18*(3), 453–468. https://doi.org/10.1007/s10984-015-9194-1

He, Y., Hutson, B. L., Elliott, M. J., & Bloom, J. L. (2016). *From departing to achieving: Keys to success for international students in U.S. colleges and universities*. Stipes Publishing L.L.C.

Heller, C. A., & Cooper-Kahn, J. (2022, April). Executive function issues and ADHD: Are they more like twins or cousins? *Attention*, 26–28. https://chadd.org/adhd-news/adhd-news-adults/executive-function-issues-and-adhd/

Hogan, K. A., & Sathy, V. (2022). *Inclusive teaching: Strategies for promoting equity in the college classroom*. West Virginia University Press.

Howlett, M. A. (2015). *Freight planning and the metropolis: The role of Metropolitan Planning Organizations in regional freight transportation planning* [PhD Thesis]. University of North Carolina at Chapel Hill. https://doi.org/10.17615/yn62-xf78

Jenkins, P. D., & Fink, J. (2015). *What we know about transfer*. Community College Research Center, Teachers College, Columbia University. https://doi.org/10.7916/D8ZG6R55

Kennedy, M. R. T. (2017). *Coaching college students with executive function problems*. The Guilford Press.

McGuire, S. Y. (2020). *Dismantling systemic racism in learning support: The time is now!* CRLA – College Reading & Learning Association. https://www.crla.net/images/icons/Miscellaneous/CRLA-Article-on-Systemic-Racism-6.15.2020-v3.pdf

Museus, S. D. (2021). Revisiting the role of academic advising in equitably serving diverse college students. *The Journal of the National Academic Advising Association*, *41*(1), 26–32. https://doi.org/10.12930/NACADA-21-06

National Research Council. (2012). *Discipline-based education research: Understanding and improving learning in undergraduate science and engineering*. The National Academies Press. https://doi.org/10.17226/13362

Parker, D. R., & Boutelle, K. (2009). Executive function coaching for college students with learning disabilities and ADHD: A new approach for fostering self-determination. *Learning Disabilities Research & Practice*, *24*(4), 204–215. https://doi.org/10.1111/j.1540-5826.2009.00294.x

Parker, D. R., Hoffman, S. F., Sawilowsky, S., & Rolands, L. (2011). An examination of the effects of ADHD coaching on university students' executive functioning. *Journal of Postsecondary Education and Disability*, *24*(2), 115–132. https://files.eric.ed.gov/fulltext/EJ943698.pdf

Powell, C., Demetriou, C., & Fisher, A. (2013). Micro-affirmations in academic advising: Small acts, big impact. *Mentor: An Academic Advising Journal*, *15*. https://doi.org/10.26209/mj1561286

Pratt, I. S., Harwood, H. B., Cavazos, J. T., & Ditzfeld, C. P. (2019). Should I stay or should I go? Retention in first-generation college students. *Journal of College Student Retention: Research, Theory & Practice*, *21*(1), 105–118. https://doi.org/10.1177/1521025117690868

Puckett, T., & Lind, N. S. (Eds.). (2020). *Cultural competence in higher education*. Emerald Publishing Limited.

Richman, E. L., Rademacher, K. N., & Maitland, T. L. (2014). Coaching and college success. *Journal of Postsecondary Education and Disability*, *27*(1), 33–50. https://files.eric.ed.gov/fulltext/EJ1029647.pdf

Rowe, M. (2008). Micro-affirmations and micro-inequities. *Journal of the International Ombudsman Association*, *1*(1), 45–48.

Saenz, V. B., Hurtado, S., Barrera, D., Wolf, D., & Yeung, F. (2007). *First in my family: A profile of first-generation college students at four-year institutions since 1971*. Higher Education Research Institute, University of California, Los Angeles.

Sheehy, B. (2016, November 29). Graduate student success: A model that works. *NACADA: Academic Advising Today*. https://nacada.ksu.edu/Resources/Academic-Advising-Today/View-Articles/Graduate-Student-Success-A-Model-that-Works.aspx

Sue, D. W., Capodilupo, C. M., Torino, G. C., Bucceri, J. M., Holder, A., Nadal, K. L., & Esquilin, M. (2007). Racial microaggressions in everyday life: Implications for clinical practice. *American Psychologist*, *62*(4), 271–286. https://doi.org/10.1037/0003-066X.62.4.271

Taylor, V. G. (2007). *The balance of rhetoric and linguistics: A study of second language writing center tutorials* [PhD Thesis]. Purdue University.

Walker, K. Y., & Okpala, C. (2017). Exploring community college students' transfer experiences and perceptions and what they believe administration can do to improve their experiences. *The Journal of Continuing Higher Education*, *65*(1), 35–44. https://doi.org/10.1080/07377363.2017.1274618

Chapter 13

Remote Learning Environments

The need for this chapter accelerated in the wake of the wide-ranging disruptions brought on by the Covid-19 pandemic in 2020. While online and distance education was booming before the pandemic, these offerings were often situated alongside traditional in-person experiences. Students could choose to enroll in an online program or to take an online class if offered at their university. Likewise, faculty and staff who taught and supported students in online programs knew they would be teaching in that format in advance. But in March 2020, the pandemic hit, and higher education immediately changed. In an incredibly brief period, faculty and staff accustomed to working with students face-to-face and in real time had to design entirely new ways of delivering services. As weeks turned into months, remote learning, once an option, became the primary mode relied on by many students and instructors alike. Whether teaching a remote class or running virtual meetings with students, many faculty and staff were suddenly navigating unchartered territory. Students also had to make significant adjustments as their modes of learning and engaging were upended in a multitude of ways.

We drafted this chapter in the spring of 2022, two years after the initial Covid-19 lockdown. As we collectively go forward in the aftermath of systemic changes brought on by the pandemic, it seems unlikely that we will ever fully revert to pre-pandemic modes of operation. In-person learning has returned to many institutions, though they may have retained aspects of virtual learning instituted during the pandemic. The landscape in higher education is still evolving. We can run meetings with students virtually or in person; the format for classes can be hybrid, where students can participate either in person or remotely, and instructors can deliver lectures synchronously or asynchronously.

Where do the principles of academic coaching fit into this evolving environment? As higher education continues to shift and adapt to the changing times, and as professionals meet and interact with students in various ways, we can creatively utilize academic coaching principles in remote learning environments.

DOI: 10.4324/9781003291879-16

COACHING SKILLS IN VIRTUAL MEETINGS

We'll start by looking at holding virtual, individual meetings with students. Before we dig in, we want to emphasize that the goals of a coaching conversation remain identical whether held in person or virtual. Virtual meetings with students are not downgraded versions of coaching conversations; in-person coaching is not necessarily better than remote. Objectively, coaching through a computer screen differs from coaching face-to-face. Still, the overall purpose is the same: facilitate a discussion with students that promotes their growth and helps them take action. While robust videoconference technology may be relatively new, a variety of college academic coaching services have been conducted remotely via telephone since the early 2000s (Bettinger & Baker, 2014; Lehan et al., 2018; Ratey & Maitland, 2001).

When a coaching conversation happens via computer screens, the coach and the student still need to take active roles, so optimizing the conditions is essential. If possible, the coach and student should situate themselves in a quiet, no- (or low-) distraction setting. While most students understand that they ought to approach a virtual meeting with a college professional the same way they approach an in-person meeting, some students might need encouragement and guidance on this front. For example, logging on to a virtual meeting with a coach while wearing pajamas in bed, seated in a noisy dining hall, or while walking across campus on the phone is suboptimal. As coaches, we want to help students understand how to make the most of their session, which includes problem-solving with them to ensure they are physically and geographically in a space conducive to coaching.

As you know by now, communication in all its forms is a critical tool of academic coaching, with listening fully—which includes paying attention to body language, tone, mood, and more—at the top of the list. All other tools flow from the ability to listen: asking open-ended questions, staying curious, articulating, reframing, and so on. For several reasons, listening fully via Zoom meetings (or via any video conferencing platform) may require extra effort. For one, access to body language is limited. Eye contact functions differently; for the most part, we see only each other's faces. The face is arguably the most crucial component of one's body language. However, when we are in the same physical with another person there is more to observe. We might notice, for example, how students enter the space and hold themselves. We might see stickers on their laptops and paraphernalia on their backpacks that give us glimpses of their personality. Messages on students' T-shirts or dress styles might also paint a fuller picture. As discussed in Chapter 5, however, we must avoid over-interpreting and making assumptions about these observations. But they can help spark our curiosity.

So, how do coaches listen fully in virtual meetings with students? When students haven't masked or blurred their screen background, coaches can pay attention to the student's environment without being nosy or intrusive. Are they at their home, in a study lounge in their residence hall, or in a secluded nook in a library? How does their environment seem to be impacting them and the session? Anything non-personal piquing a coach's interest might serve to generate curious questions. An innocuous question about something noticeable in their space might help to put a new student at ease and might allow for a few moments of chit-chat to build rapport and warm up the session. "Cool poster!" or "A cat! What's the name?" or "Looks like your sitting outside on a beautiful day." When students choose to keep their backgrounds blurred or off, coaches respect their choice and turn their efforts to listen fully without using those visual clues.

To make up for some of the potential communication barriers associated with virtual meetings, coaches might need to verbally check in with students even more than they would for in-person meetings. Sprinkling in simple questions throughout a session gives the coach and student a chance to recalibrate if necessary. Here are a few examples: "How are you doing so far?" "Before we continue, what thoughts or questions do you have?" or "Let's pause for a check-in; anything you want to review?" Of course, these questions are also helpful for in-person meetings, but they might be even more vital during virtual meetings due to reduced access to body language.

Managing self is another critically important coaching skill. Academic coaches must learn to continually manage themselves in their conversations with students—attend to their own distracting thoughts, judgments, assumptions, etc.—to ensure they are providing the most effective coaching. Coaching through a computer screen offers new opportunities to refine self-management skills. Our physical environment matters more than ever to help us stay focused and locked into an online conversation. For example, computer notifications that appear or make audible sounds while working with a student are likely distracting. Same with our seemingly ubiquitous cell phones. It's probably a good idea to turn off computer notifications, close email programs, and silence phones (or at least move them out of sight to avoid possible interruptions from text messages, calls, and other alerts) so that we can be present and listen fully.

Many college professionals worked from home during at least part of the pandemic. For many, work from home has continued to some degree. Running virtual meetings with students from our home environment might offer more self-management practice. Depending on temperament, some may find it challenging to maintain a work frame of mind when immersed in the place where we live our personal lives. Some of us deal with literal space issues, like finding a quiet place to work when sharing our homes with spouses, children, and pets. Some of us encounter logistical problems with internet connectivity when bandwidth is compromised. Self-management in these scenarios is essential to clear the proverbial decks and be present and available to the students with whom we work. However, depending on the campus work context, remote academic coaching may bolster our ability to listen fully if our remote environment is quieter and less chaotic than an in-person setting.

COACHING SKILLS IN ASYNCHRONOUS INTERACTIONS

Incorporating academic coaching principles can make interactions richer for classes or meetings that are asynchronous in format—meaning that the professional and student are not interacting in real time.

One-on-One Meetings

Let's start by looking at asynchronous, one-on-one meetings. Some departments on college campuses had already been offering this format of working with students before Covid-19 with asynchronous writing conferences being a notable example (Abels, 2006; Funt, 2019; Hewett, 2015; Peguesse, 2013; Raign, 2013). As higher education continues to adapt to the changes wrought by Covid, asynchronous meetings with students are more commonplace. The general idea of asynchronous meetings is that students and staff communicate via writing on a digital platform, such as online portals, email, or a learning management system. To make these interactions more effective, students often respond to a series of prepared prompts and leave a document for feedback. Later, staff can then respond in writing to the student.

Prompts aligned with academic coaching principles will enhance the experience for the student. Good coaching questions provoke thinking and reflection, whether asked aloud in a conversation or presented in writing. As Michael Bungay Stanier, author of *The Coaching Habit*, notes, "Questions work just as well typed as they do spoken" (2016, p. 204). Some students might prefer responding to written prompts because they benefit from the extra processing time that might not be possible in a real-time dialogue. A research study we participated in suggested that asynchronous online academic coaching could yield both similar effects and student satisfaction to synchronous in-person academic coaching (Howlett et al., 2021).

Here are sample coaching-infused prompts that fit in the world of academic support, career services, and academic advising:

1. For students seeking writing support for a paper:
   - "What do you think are the strengths of your paper, and what are your concerns?"
   - "What particular writing skill or topic would you like feedback on?"
   - "What is your goal with your introduction (or conclusion)?"

2. For students seeking general academic support:
   - "What topic would you like us to focus on today? (For example, time management or study strategies?)"
   - "So far, what has been going well (regarding the topic), and what has been challenging?"
   - "What would progress look like?"
   - "What are one or two steps you could take now to move forward? What resources might help you?"
3. For students seeking feedback on a resume:
   - "What's your overall impression of your resume?"
   - "What skills do you have that you want to make sure you highlight?"
   - "If there's a part of your resume that you're concerned about, what is it and why?"
   - "What particular feedback are you looking for?"
   - "What do you want the reader to know about you as a candidate?"
4. For students wanting feedback from an academic adviser about selecting a major:
   - "When you think about taking the classes required for a possible major in _____, what excites you? What are you eager to learn?"
   - "How does this major align with your strengths and interests?"
   - "What skills do you already have to help you succeed in this major? What support might you need?"
   - "What do you understand about this major's prerequisites and degree requirements?"

Incorporating academic coaching principles into asynchronous interactions relies heavily on asking open-ended questions. It bears repeating that open-ended questions are powerful for students and all of us. The creative thinking and discernment they provoke can sometimes reveal answers we already possess or ideas we didn't know we had. When we can access our wisdom and discover insights into ourselves, we benefit from more reflective decision-making, greater confidence, and improved resourcefulness. Pondering open-ended questions is certainly not the only way to achieve personal growth—far from it!—but it is one way. However, rarely do we pose thought-provoking questions to ourselves. Therefore, professionals working with college students can play an important role in helping promote their growth by instilling thought-provoking questions into their conversations.

Recorded Lectures

Some instructors record their lectures ahead of or instead of meeting with their class. Some do so when teaching in active-learning classrooms (where students view the recording before gathering for class), and some do so for courses that are entirely online. What follows are suggestions to integrate academic coaching principles into these scenarios.

- At the start of the recording, invite students to prepare themselves with suggestions such as: "How do you imagine the focus of our last lecture will inform today's?" or "What might be a few reasons I assigned you the reading for today's lecture?"
- Include a couple of pauses during the recording where you ask students to respond to questions like, "What do you think is the most important piece we've covered so far?" or "What part brings up the most questions for you?" or "What surprises you?"
- After the lecture, leave students with ideas to consider, such as: "How does today's lecture fit into the overall class objectives?" or "How would you summarize today's lecture in just a handful of sentences?" or "What follow-up questions do you have?"

Online Forums

Online forums are commonly used features within learning management systems. They provide students and instructors opportunities to engage in writing with one another via discussion threads and often become the centerpiece of online learning (Darby & Lang, 2019). These forums are an excellent device to embed coaching principles and encourage students to use them with each other. For example, the guidelines instructors set for students could include a direction to write the first posting in the thread as an open-ended question for everyone to ponder. The instructor could encourage students to use coaching-type skills when responding to the thread, such as reframing, articulation, and bottom-lining. By exposing students to coaching principles, students may begin to adopt them elsewhere in their academic lives.

Instructors set the tone of an online forum to maximize student engagement. The design of academic coaching promotes critical thinking and reflection, so when instructors embed the pedagogical underpinnings of coaching into their forum contributions, they foster student engagement that can be robust and stimulating. Therefore, in addition to encouraging students to embrace coaching language, instructors should also model this language themselves. Possible examples of online forum interactions that incorporate an academic coaching orientation include:

- "I'm curious about Jamie's last point. Can he explain more about his idea?" Or "Who might be able to articulate a point of view similar to Jamie's?"

- "I'd like to reframe the idea about XXX to YYY. I invite you to present an argument that either agrees or disagrees with this reframing."
- "I want to acknowledge Ken for tying two complicated ideas together."
- "How do you think the readings I assigned this week relate to the overall course objectives?"

Coaching Skills in Synchronous Classes with Remote Components

As described in Chapter 10, instructors can incorporate academic coaching principles into their teaching and curriculum. It's worth a brief examination about how to utilize coaching skills advantageously in an educational landscape that now routinely includes synchronous instruction that can be entirely virtual or where student attendance is hybrid (some attend in-person and some attend remotely).

Teaching via a video-conferencing platform like Zoom comes with benefits when instructors use additional program features. Live chat and breakout rooms are two tools in Zoom that can be particularly useful when facilitating a class; they can also increase student engagement. Instructors can pose open-ended coaching questions in the chat box (and aloud when teaching a hybrid class) and encourage written responses. Some students who might be reticent to speak aloud in an in-person class could prefer contributing via the chat feature. The chat box provides more than one way for students to contribute to the class which can increase overall participation and align with many of the principles of universal design in education. In essence, by broadening the modes of communication and delivery—whether from the instructor's or student's standpoint—the overall educational experience is more inclusive and accessible.

Breakout rooms are another handy tool in video-conferencing platforms that give instructors and students a venue to use coaching tools. Whether teaching in-person or remotely, breaking students into groups can be useful for many reasons. Breakout groups allow students to engage actively in the material with their peers. Instructors can foster a productive environment for breakout groups, similar to promoting effective online forums, when they set the stage for students. Again, finding opportunities to utilize coaching skills can enhance the experience for students. Instructors can send students attending class remotely to breakout rooms with open-ended questions to consider or concepts to reframe. They can broadcast written coaching-type messages related to the class content into the breakout rooms for students to discuss. They can encourage students to use the chat feature in the breakout rooms to promote additional written reflection among group members.

WRAPPING UP

Online and remote learning was instituted long before the Covid-19 pandemic, allowing more students to access educational opportunities. Still, the pandemic was an impetus for colleges and universities to further expand the modes of engaging with students, forcing us to introduce additional remote options in the way we structure meetings and class experiences. From holding virtual and asynchronous meetings with students, to providing recorded lectures as an additional resource for students, to running hybrid classes, and to enriching the use and expectations of online forums, faculty and staff accustomed to in-person work have needed to adopt at least some elements of remote work into their interactions with students. Now that we're several years beyond the start of Covid-19, we can reflect on the changes adopted, and we can consider how to go forward. By remembering the fundamental beliefs of academic coaching—coaches collaborate with students who are already capable and competent with ample self-knowledge, and they can grow through challenges—remote interactions can be equally powerful as in-person interactions. By using the fundamental tools of asking open-ended questions while listening with curiosity and managing self, staff and faculty can facilitate meaningful and effective interactions with students regardless of the modality. In short, applying the principles of academic coaching to remote interactions with students makes good sense and can enhance the experience for all.

REFERENCES

Abels, K. T. (2006). The Writing Center at the University of North Carolina at Chapel Hill: A site and story under construction. In C. Murphy & B. L. Stay (Eds.), *The writing center director's resource book* (pp. 393–402). Taylor & Francis.

Bettinger, E. P., & Baker, R. B. (2014). The effects of student coaching: An evaluation of a randomized experiment in student advising. *Educational Evaluation and Policy Analysis, 36*(1), 3–19. https://doi.org/10.3102/0162373713500523

Darby, F., & Lang, J. M. (2019). *Small teaching online: Applying learning science in online classes.* John Wiley & Sons.

Funt, A. (2019). *In favor of a minimalist, asynchronous online approach to coaching multiliteracies in a traditional writing center* [PhD Thesis]. University of North Carolina at Chapel Hill. https://doi.org/10.17615/jj0q-ps80

Hewett, B. L. (2015). *The online writing conference: A guide for teachers and tutors.* Bedford/St. Martin's.

Howlett, M. A., McWilliams, M. A., Rademacher, K., O'Neill, J. C., Maitland, T. L., Abels, K., Demetriou, C., & Panter, A. T. (2021). Investigating the effects of academic coaching on college students' metacognition. *Innovative Higher Education, 46*(2), 189–204. https://doi.org/10.1007/s10755-020-09533-7

Lehan, T. J., Hussey, H. D., & Shriner, M. (2018). The influence of academic coaching on persistence in online graduate students. *Mentoring & Tutoring: Partnership in Learning*, *26*(3), 289–304. https://doi.org/10.1080/13611267.2018.1511949

Peguesse, C. L. (2013). Assessing the effectiveness of tutor comments in email sessions. *Journal of College Reading and Learning*, *44*(1), 95–104. https://doi.org/10.1080/1 0790195.2013.10850375

Raign, K. R. (2013). Creating verbal immediacy – The use of immediacy and avoidance techniques in online tutorials. *Praxis: A Writing Center Journal*, *10*(2). https://repositories.lib.utexas.edu/handle/2152/62181

Ratey, N. A., & Maitland, T. L. (2001). Working with an ADD coach. In P. O. Quinn (Ed.), *ADD and the college student: A guide for high school and college students with attention deficit disorder* (Rev. ed., pp. 99–108). Magination Press.

Stanier, M. B. (2016). *The coaching habit: Say less, ask more & change the way you lead forever.* Box of Crayons Press.

Part IV

Next Steps

Chapter 14

Implementing Academic Coaching

As you come to the final chapter of the book, we hope you are motivated and inspired to start experimenting with academic coaching. Regardless of who you are—a newly hired coach preparing to work with college students for the first time, a staff or faculty member looking for ways to improve the effectiveness of your interactions with students, a seasoned coach needing a refresher, or part of a team charged with creating or expanding an existing coaching program—this chapter is geared to help you plan concrete next steps.

You'll likely notice how this chapter mirrors the last phase of academic coaching: design and commit to plans. And you'll notice checkpoints along the way for you to do just that. We'll provide plenty of ideas, but as is the case when we coach students, we encourage you to tailor them to fit your needs and goals.

Let's get started!

GROWING AS AN ACADEMIC COACH

You may already be employed at a college or university as an academic coach or in a position with many similarities. You may be new to the field, or you may have been doing this type of work for years. As has been the refrain in this book, there's always the ability to learn, grow, and improve. We expect that from our students. We must expect that about ourselves.

One of the benefits of being in an academic coaching position is that there will be plenty of opportunities to practice and implement portions of this book. You'll likely find it helpful to take time to reflect on where you are in terms of coaching as well as considering your professional goals. Think through your experiences with coaching and reflect on questions like these:

- What are your strengths? What are some growth opportunities?
- What can you do to make your work even more beneficial to students? What common pitfalls may you encounter when working with students?

DOI: 10.4324/9781003291879-18   **161**

- If you go on professional autopilot, what does that look like? What are your blind spots? Where might some of your personal lenses and perspectives potentially influence your work with students?
- What should you celebrate about your coaching?
- What helps you stay student-centered? What detracts from your student-centered work?
- What are some additional reflection questions that would be helpful to ask yourself?

Your reflection can be done in several ways: by writing, chatting with someone else, thinking, drawing, and so on. Be creative!

Instead of a narrative approach to self-reflecting and learning, you can also take a more quantitative or formal approach. You might rank the ten expanded skills from Chapter 7 in the order you are most comfortable with. You can also create or borrow a rubric to assess your own academic coaching. Recording videos of yourself coaching can be especially useful in this regard (Funt & Esposito, 2019; Hall, 2017).

As an academic coach, there will be multiple ways to build targeted practice into your professional work. One classic method is to brainstorm open-ended questions that you find especially impactful. Remember that these questions don't need to be extensive to be powerful. In fact, their power often grows as their length decreases. "What's next?" is a great example of a brief but potent question.

Another popular approach to grow your skills is to select an area of focus for a defined period of time. Choose something from the academic coaching model and practice with it for a week or any time frame that you'd like. It could be a phase like set the agenda or an expanded skill like bottom line. Targeted, intentional practice will benefit your work as a higher education coach.

INCORPORATING ACADEMIC COACHING INTO OTHER PROFESSIONAL CONTEXTS

Even if you are not interested in becoming an academic coach, or you serve in a different professional capacity, we believe that academic coaching principles, tools, methods, and approaches can be applicable to a wide variety of higher education professional contexts (see Chapters 10 and 11). If you are a faculty or a university staff member, you've likely already reflected on the similarities and differences between a coach approach and how you typically work with college students. But like the ending of an academic coaching appointment, we invite you to translate some of your ideas and brainstorms into more concrete plans of action.

One next step that is available to anyone, whether a newcomer to this world or one with decades of coaching experience, is to be more intentional in your interactions and work with students. Even the most committed of us can understandably settle into routines and patterns. Working in higher education can be an exhausting enterprise. Professionals in all industries and career types can benefit from periodically taking stock, reflecting, and resetting in terms of intentional actions. Being intentional is one way to avoid falling into professional autopilot.

When incorporating elements of academic coaching into your work, being intentional can take multiple forms. Staff and faculty who have attended academic coaching trainings frequently leave with the goal of asking more open-ended questions in their student conversations. They also begin to make more concerted efforts to have students leave meetings with action plans that were developed collaboratively (Howlett et al., 2021). Another frequent goal is to restrain from sharing ideas or suggestions and, instead, start with the student's ideas.

Another form of being more intentional with students is to recenter yourself before student meetings or classes. Even setting aside a moment or two to slow down, breathe, and reflect can be beneficial. Pausing to think, "I'm about to talk with [student's name] who has their own history, present, and future. Who has their own goals, dreams, worries, obstacles, opportunities, and thoughts" can be a powerful strategy for student-centered work. The same can be done for classes. Consider the difference between preparing to teach a class and saying to yourself "just another class" and "this is a unique group of individuals who are capable and competent."

In addition to practicing greater intentionality in your student interactions, you can apply elements of academic coaching to multiple contexts, settings, and roles. It might be useful for you to think of the range and modes of interactions that you have with students (and, indeed, other people) where aspects of the academic coaching model may be applicable. Here's a beginning list:

- Facilitating office hours
- Supervising student employees
- Teaching classes
- Communicating via email or digital learning platforms
- Advising students (as academic advisors, career counselors, thesis advisors, and so on)

We fully recognize that an academic coaching approach may not be the best match for every situation or context, but we encourage you to consider aspects of your professional work where academic coaching might be a good fit. Once you've identified an area, take a moment to think through how you could apply elements of academic coaching to your work in the near future.

BUILDING ON EXISTING ACADEMIC COACHING PROGRAMS

Many colleges and universities already offer academic coaching in some form. As we know, there is no one agreed-upon definition of academic coaching, and there is no one agreed-upon form of delivery. And that's okay! We also value the overlap between academic coaching with other inquiry-based models of working with students, such as appreciative advising (Bloom et al., 2008, 2014) and motivational interviewing (Miller & Rollnick, 2012).

For those with existing academic coaching programs or programs adjacent to academic coaching, we hope this book has given you plenty of information to think about as you imagine how you want your program to expand and grow. As a starting place, we encourage you to identify concepts or skills we covered that are particularly interesting to you and your colleagues. Along the same lines, you can also identify which areas of your program seem in need of strengthening or if there are gaps in your program altogether. By articulating how ideas from this book might address a need in your work with students, you can start to make meaningful changes to your program.

Here are some examples of how you might approach identifying needs in your current program:

- If your students don't seem invested in the conversation or appear to be responding how they think you want them to, consider tweaking your program to guide students toward setting their own agenda for the session.
- If your students aren't following through with plans discussed in a session, maybe your program would benefit from greater emphasis on designing accountability plans.
- If your sessions seem akin to consulting because staff primarily offer advice, you might aim to include significantly more open-ended questions in your conversations. Remarkable shifts can happen between a student and a coach with greater use of this powerful coaching tool.
- If your sessions seem to drift from topic to topic, adopting a few expanded coaching skills, such as take charge, hold the focus, and bottom line, could be helpful.
- If your academic coaches are working with students in varying ways without a unified overarching pedagogy or structure to a coaching conversation, you might seek to standardize the overall approach for your program while maintaining the individualized, student-centered nature of the service.

164

- If your academic coaches haven't examined or reflected on their own practices recently, you could use ideas, concepts, strategies, and tools from this book to structure professional development opportunities.
- How well can you explain and describe academic coaching to a senior university administrator? If this task is challenging, you could dedicate time to identifying the primary objectives of your program and how they are achieved in your day-to-day work.

STARTING A NEW ACADEMIC COACHING PROGRAM

Starting any new educational program can be daunting. The essential elements required to create a program from the ground up are often in short supply: time and resources. Additionally, progress toward launching a new program can depend on the staff's mindset.

Some staff might be all-in with the notion of exploring and perhaps adopting academic coaching, while others may be reticent. Reluctance can be due to skepticism about the merit of academic coaching. Doubt is not necessarily problematic; it is a wise staff who thinks critically before considering program changes. Asking questions, seeking evidence, and even exploring alternatives should be encouraged for staff who aren't convinced that embracing academic coaching is the best move.

Sometimes, staff reluctance can be due to general resistance to change. Not everyone is enthusiastic to learn new things! Changing one's standard approaches—within and outside of the professional arena—takes effort and can be uncomfortable. In other words, temperament plays a role in the levels of enthusiasm staff might have when considering a new way of working with students.

Whether staff might have doubts about academic coaching or are simply resistant to change, it's important to proceed in a manner that respectfully builds buy-in. Using academic coaching principles and skills in conversations with staff makes good sense here. The essence of coaching is a collaboration that ultimately empowers the coachee to grow and make changes. When beginning to design a new coaching program, the same goal applies to staff, so carefully consider how to engage them in the new venture to help them feel empowered, capable of, and excited for growth.

A first consideration in creating a coaching program is determining who might serve as academic coaches: full-time staff, external coaches, graduate students, or undergrads serving as peer coaches?

The provision of academic coaching can take a variety of forms. We see many benefits for having dedicated, trained, and specialized staff, and we also recognize that colleges and universities may not have the ability or resources to primarily employ staff as academic coaches. There are also benefits from employing graduate students and designing peer-to-peer coaching programs in a university setting.

Let's briefly look at peer coaches. Colleges have been developing and expanding peer-to-peer services for a multiplicity of reasons. Strengths of such programs include the potential of removing barriers to access and increasing relational support (Grabsch et al., 2021; Simmons & Smith, 2020; Talbot et al., 2015; Warner et al., 2018). Aligning with the definition of academic coaching being a collaborative relationship, Parker, Hall, and Kram argue that "the unique contribution of peer coaching is the inherent mutuality and reciprocity of the process. Both individuals are learners, in contrast to more traditional models of mentoring and other hierarchical learning relationships" (2008, p. 490). Challenges with peer-to-peer academic support can include difficulty in clearly defining roles, establishing boundaries, and navigating issues of power (Colvin & Ashman, 2010). Peer coaches may also find difficulty in working with students with complex needs, especially since academic coaching is typically much broader in scope than a service like peer tutoring.

In thinking about an academic coaching program that includes student coaches, whether they are advanced graduate students or undergraduates functioning in a peer-to-peer role, it is helpful to consider a few questions. Of course, no matter what configuration your institution takes when it comes to providing academic coaching, active reflection and evaluation will help improve the overall program's success.

- How will student employees be supervised?
- What are the benefits and potential risks of academic coaching delivered by students?
- How will the student coaches refer to and connect with other campus resources in situations that move beyond the bounds of their roles?

Regardless of who will provide academic coaching—full-time staff, graduate students, or undergraduates—they will need to be trained, which is where we will turn next. Although the need for training may seem obvious, many higher education academic coaches receive little or no training for their campus roles (Sepulveda, 2017).

TRAINING: FIRST CONSIDERATIONS

The components of effective and engaging training activities will depend on several factors: staff size and readiness, available time, and the amount of academic coaching content necessary to meet the training goals for your program and staff. The following questions will help you begin shaping the experience:

1. Can you devote dedicated staff time to training?
2. How many total hours can you allocate for training?
3. What size group will you have?

Let's Look at Each Factor

Dedicated Staff Time for Training

An ideal training scenario would be where staff clear their calendars for blocks of time to convene and focus on training as a team. A set-up like this is basically a version of a classroom which can be advantageous because everyone is learning the same thing simultaneously. Staff also benefit when they can learn from each other, have real-time discussions about how academic coaching works and what it might look like in their department, and think through questions and concerns together. Additionally, when staff can fully participate rather than toggle back and forth between training and job responsibilities, getting everyone on the same page about academic coaching may be easier.

That said, we know that carving out time to gather staff for dedicated chunks of time may be difficult. For student-facing offices, it can seem nearly impossible to find time to assemble as a group that won't interfere with serving students. Summer can be a convenient time to schedule training opportunities if the pace of serving students slows down and can allow for robust professional development. If your staff convenes for regular, recurring meetings throughout the semester or year, reserving meetings for training activities is another option.

When the reality is that your staff is unable to gather as a group for training activities—or if you are the sole staff person in your office—self-directed activities could be used instead and completed individually or in pairs. Activities can include reading, reflecting, practicing coaching conversations, and interacting in an online forum as staff work through the exercises. Expanding one's learning by reflecting on and then building upon prior experiences is a cornerstone of adult learning theory (Cox, 2015).

Total Hours to Allocate for Training

In shaping a training experience, another factor is determining the number of hours to allocate. Here are two questions to ponder when thinking about this:

1. What are your academic coaching training goals, and how much time will you need to meet them?
2. How much time can you realistically allocate for training, and how will that shape your goals?

In the first question, the assumption is that time (more or less) is not the driving factor or is at least not a major barrier in designing training experiences. You have a wide-open canvas to develop a series of activities that provide staff with the level of academic skill-building you'd like.

In the second question, the amount of available time determines the breadth and depth of the training.

When committing to significant amounts of time is not possible or perhaps not of interest for departments or groups, it is still feasible to design meaningful activities for staff that will set a solid foundation of academic coaching skills.

Size of the Group

Learning to facilitate academic coaching conversations successfully is contingent on practicing coaching conversations. Literally! Reading about academic coaching and observing a coaching conversation is helpful, but jumping in and trying it out is essential. Imagine trying to learn tennis by only watching instructional videos; getting on a court and hitting a ball with a racket is when tennis skills start to develop. Similarly, when you sit across from someone and lead them through the phases of a coaching session, coaching skills develop. Practice is a cornerstone of active learning environments for college students (Baepler et al., 2016; Hogan & Sathy, 2022), and it's also the foundation for effective training and professional development. Therefore, when thinking about staff training, you must think about how to optimize a group size that provides opportunities for people to practice coaching conversations. Ideally, your group would allow for a few different partnership configurations, so staff have more opportunities to learn from each other. If it's only feasible to form a group of just a few people, that is okay, too. You and your colleagues will still learn.

TRAINING TEMPLATES AND ACTIVITIES

After you've thought through staff training configurations and available time, you are ready to create a training template. We've provided four templates based on how much you can allocate. As you review them, you'll notice that the more time you have, more of the academic coaching model and coaching skills can be covered and practiced. These templates are suggestions and can be tailored to meet the unique needs and goals of your group. At the end of this section, you'll find a list of suggested activities to help you get started.

Training Templates

One to Three Available Hours

When only a short time frame is available, such as a few hours, your goal could be to provide an overview of the following:

- The academic coaching definition

- The fundamental coaching beliefs
- The fundamental coaching tool of asking open-ended questions
- The four phases of a coaching conversation (brief introduction)

In addition to reviewing the foundational elements of academic coaching listed above, it would be necessary to provide an opportunity for staff to practice coaching. Form partners to experiment with short coaching conversations—a few minutes each is fine—where the coach tries to ask only open-ended questions.

While a few hours of academic coaching training is undoubtedly brief, participants can leave with a sense of the essence of the model, a great beginning. A meaningful shift in working with students can occur by adopting the belief that coaching is collaborative and that students are fundamentally competent, and by adopting the practice of asking more open-ended questions. Sharing the structure of the four phases is important even in a brief training because it gives staff an anchor in facilitating a conversation.

Four to Eight Hours

A half or full day of training can allow staff to dive into more pieces of the academic coaching model. Goals for a training of this length could include outlining the following:

- The academic coaching definition
- The fundamental coaching beliefs
- **ALL** the fundamental coaching tools
- The four phases of a coaching conversation in greater detail

As mentioned already, reserving time for practicing coaching is always crucial in any length of professional development. With a four-to-eight-hour time frame, it is possible to arrange several practices. And by adding in an overview of each fundamental coaching tool (asking open-ended questions, and listening fully, being curious, and managing self), participants have more skills to practice when working with partners. The extra time can also give participants more than one coaching practice—and lengthier practices at that—and an opportunity to move through each phase of a conversation (set the agenda, self-reflect and learn, explore options and actions, and design and commit to plans).

A half or full day of training activities moves staff beyond exposure to the fundamentals of academic coaching toward a more grounded understanding of how to better use the tools to facilitate entire coaching conversations.

Up to Two Days

Up to two days of training moves staff to a deeper understanding of the academic coaching model and gives them more tools to use in various situations. Goals for a training of this length could include covering and practicing the following:

- The academic coaching definition
- The fundamental coaching beliefs
- The fundamental coaching tools
- The four phases of a coaching conversation
- The expanded academic coaching skills
- Coaching topics

The addition of expanded coaching skills gives staff a broader range of options in facilitating an academic coaching conversation. By strategically employing expanded skills such as championing or taking charge, a coach both individualizes a coaching conversation and enhances the coaching's effectiveness.

An effective coach is versatile and can work with a student on issues around time management, reading, academic eligibility, and more. We provide example training activities for some of these topics later in this chapter. The extra time in training that might run for two days helps develop versatile coaches because they allow for discussions and coaching practices focused on various topics and situations students might bring to a conversation.

Staff who can set aside closer to two days of academic coaching training will leave with a more enriched skill set. We put a premium on coaching practice; the more time allocated for training activities, the more practice is possible, and the more confident and skillful staff can become.

Two or More Days

When staff wants to fully commit to building an academic coaching program, allocating more than two days of training is the way to go. The robust list of goals below lays the groundwork for the full implementation of academic coaching as described in this book. Please note that even with several days of training—a significant time commitment—continual practice and reflection are needed for a coach to reach high levels of proficiency. Becoming an effective academic coach takes time and practice.

- The academic coaching definition
- The fundamental coaching beliefs
- The fundamental coaching tools
- The expanded coaching skills

- The phases of a coaching conversation
- Coaching topics
- Coaching with diverse populations

Including the goal of coaching diverse populations of students makes a multi-day training especially valuable. As discussed in Chapter 12, a coach will be more effective when aware of and sensitive to students as unique people with unique needs. A multi-day training allows staff to experiment with coaching skills applicable when working with a range of students. For example, coaching a first-generation first-year college student will likely require different academic coaching skills compared with coaching a senior college student newly diagnosed with ADHD.

A multi-day training provides staff with each important piece of the academic coaching model. Assembling the pieces into a cohesive picture takes time to complete and will look different depending on the group, the department, and the institution. However, exposure and practice with each piece of the coaching model will give staff the essential components of a solid academic coaching program.

Activities

When designing a training experience that adequately prepares staff to coach, we believe a mix of content delivery, coaching demonstrations (whether live or from recorded sessions), and coaching practice is critical. When learning a new skill, whether a sport, a musical instrument, or calculus, a beneficial process would include an explanation or description of the skill (content delivery), a demonstration of the skill, and the chance to practice the skill with guidance and feedback. We suggest the same principles when designing an academic coaching training.

Another layer of planning is considering how to mix up the activities to allow staff to participate as a whole group, in small groups or partners, and individually. A variety of activities serve the needs of different learners and temperaments. We know that a small staff limits the amount of different partner and group combinations, and that's okay. The most important part of designing activities that prepare staff to use academic coaching skills is practice. As long as a staff has at least two members, taking time to practice coaching can and should be included.

Consider the examples of training exercises below as frameworks for you to build from as you design activities that meet the goals and needs of your staff. Note that the examples assume that they have been preceded by a discussion around the fundamental coaching beliefs and coaching tools.

Developing Coaching Skills for Study Strategy Support

- For students wanting to improve their reading effectiveness (or studying for a STEM class, or note-taking, and so on), ask staff to generate open-ended questions a coach might ask to better understand the student's situation.
- Collect the open-ended questions in a list that everyone can view and use for the practice activity.
- Ask staff to share resources and strategies that might be useful for a student wanting to improve their reading effectiveness.
- Next, ask staff to brainstorm the language and approaches they might use with a student in which they share resources in a collaborative, non-didactic manner.
- Partner up and practice! One partner plays the coach, while the other roleplays a student wanting to improve their reading effectiveness.

Developing Coaching Skills for Support on Transitioning to College

- Ask staff to generate a list of challenges students might face when entering college for the first time.
- Ask staff to list skills new students would likely need to develop to ease their transition.
- Next, invite staff to draft open-ended coaching questions that would be useful in identifying skills students have and skills they need.
- Partner up and practice! Same as above: one staff member coaches another staff member who is role-playing a new student.

Developing Coaching Skills for Support around Academic Eligibility

- Invite staff to imagine the reasons behind a student's struggle with academic eligibility and the feelings that might accompany these challenges.
- Review the five fundamental coaching beliefs with staff and ask how they could engage with the student through the filter of each belief. For example, ask staff to arrive at coaching questions that underscore the belief that the focus of the conversation is the student, not the problem, or that students are the experts in their lives.
- Partner up and practice! Ask the staff person playing the coach to focus their questions that match just one coaching belief.

As we approach the final section of the book, it's time for a classic coaching question:

WHAT'S NEXT?

Coaching is about taking action. It's our sincere wish that you move beyond reading this book and incorporate elements of academic coaching into your work. Just as we coach students to design and commit to plans, we encourage the same for you. Are you ready?

Start drafting an action plan and be clear on your tangible next steps. Reflect on how taking these next steps will help you move forward with your professional goals. What kinds of accountability structures might support you in implementing your plans? How will you evaluate your progress?

We talk frequently with students about the iterative nature of academic coaching. Students develop action plans, go out and implement them to varying degrees, see what happens, learn from the experience, revise their approaches and strategies, move forward, and repeat. As academic coaches, we help facilitate these steps and over time they translate into academic growth and development.

The same cyclical and iterative processes are applicable to you. Whether you're expanding academic coaching, starting a new academic coaching program, getting training on becoming an academic coach, furthering your professional development, or incorporating elements of academic coaching into your professional work, we believe that the overarching goal is long-term growth and development. If you're using ideas and strategies from this book and applying them to your work in higher education there's a reasonable chance that everything might not work perfectly the first time. That's fine. In fact, if you don't run into a few rough edges, that's likely a sign that you need to engage in the learning process even more. We regularly work on many of the topics covered within the pages of this book, despite decades of experience as higher education academic coaches.

This final section of the final chapter of the book isn't merely hypothetical; it is directed to you, the reader. It's one thing to read about academic coaching, and it's another thing to literally change one or more aspects of your professional work. The ideas in this chapter should give you a good starting point, so we encourage you to jump in and try out a few of them. The risks are likely low and the potential rewards for you and your students will be high. And, as we routinely tell our students, little tweaks lead to big changes.

REFERENCES

Baepler, P., Walker, J., Brooks, D. C., Saichaie, K., & Petersen, C. I. (2016). *A guide to teaching in the active learning classroom: History, research, and practice*. Stylus Publishing, LLC.

Bloom, J. L., Hutson, B. L., & He, Y. (2008). *The appreciative advising revolution*. Stipes Publishing L.L.C.

Bloom, J. L., Hutson, B. L., He, Y., & Konkle, E. (2014). *The appreciative advising revolution training workbook: Translating theory to practice.* Stipes Publishing L.L.C.

Colvin, J. W., & Ashman, M. (2010). Roles, risks, and benefits of peer mentoring relationships in higher education. *Mentoring & Tutoring: Partnership in Learning,* *18*(2), 121–134.

Cox, E. (2015). Coaching and adult learning: Theory and practice. *New Directions for Adult and Continuing Education,* *2015*(148), 27–38. https://doi.org/10.1002/ace.20149

Funt, A., & Esposito, S. (2019). Video recording in the writing center. *WLN: A Journal of Writing Center Scholarship,* *43*(5), 2–10.

Grabsch, D. K., Peña, R. A., & Parks, K. J. (2021). Expectations of students participating in voluntary peer academic coaching. *Journal of College Reading and Learning,* *51*(2), 95–109. https://doi.org/10.1080/10790195.2020.1798827

Hall, R. M. (2017). *Around the texts of writing center work: An inquiry-based approach to tutor education.* Utah State University Press.

Hogan, K. A., & Sathy, V. (2022). *Inclusive teaching: Strategies for promoting equity in the college classroom.* West Virginia University Press.

Howlett, M. A., McWilliams, M. A., Rademacher, K., Maitland, T. L., O'Neill, J. C., Abels, K., Demetriou, C., & Panter, A. (2021). An academic coaching training program for university professionals: A mixed methods examination. *Journal of Student Affairs Research and Practice,* *58*(3), 335–349. https://doi.org/10.1080/19496591.2020.1784750

Miller, W. R., & Rollnick, S. (2012). *Motivational interviewing: Helping people change* (3rd ed.). Guilford Press.

Parker, P., Hall, D. T., & Kram, K. E. (2008). Peer coaching: A relational process for accelerating career learning. *Academy of Management Learning & Education,* *7*(4), 487–503. https://doi.org/10.5465/amle.2008.35882189

Sepulveda, A. (2017). Exploring the roles and responsibilities of academic coaches in higher education. *Journal of Student Affairs,* *26,* 69–81.

Simmons, R., & Smith, K. S. (2020). Success central: Addressing the persistence of African-American and Latinx college students using a peer success coaching intervention. *Innovative Higher Education,* *45*(5), 419–434. https://doi.org/10.1007/s10755-020-09516-8

Talbot, R. M., Hartley, L. M., Marzetta, K., & Wee, B. S. (2015). Transforming undergraduate science education with learning assistants: Student satisfaction in large-enrollment courses. *Journal of College Science Teaching,* *44*(5), 24–30. https://www.jstor.org/stable/43631844

Warner, Z., Neater, W., Clark, L., & Lee, J. (2018). Peer coaching and motivational interviewing in postsecondary settings: Connecting retention theory with practice. *Journal of College Reading and Learning,* *48*(3), 159–174. https://doi.org/10.1080/10790195.2018.1472940

Index

Note: Page numbers followed by "n" denote endnotes.

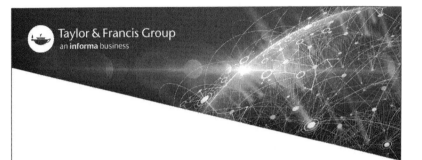

Made in the USA
Middletown, DE
15 August 2023